NURTURING THE VAGUS NERVE

The Ultimate Guide to Relieve Anxiety and Promote Wellness

By

Keri Korus
OMA International Publications

Table of Contents

INTRODUCTION

Hey there! Imagine your body has a special friend named Vagus nerve. It's like a tiny superhero inside you that can help you feel less stressed and more relaxed. I have been a massage therapist for the last fourteen years and have worked side by side with a chiropractor for over eight years. Together, we discovered how important this nerve is for reducing anxiety and making us feel better.

The Vagus Nerve is not just another part of our human anatomy. It is, in fact, a significant contributor to our overall wellness. It's akin to a superhighway, connecting our brain to many major organs in our body, controlling and influencing a variety of functions from digestion to heart rate.

But more importantly, I uncovered its central role in managing stress and anxiety. In our fast-paced, 24/7 connected world, stress is an unwelcome yet constant companion for many of us. And here was this nerve, this hidden gem, with the power to help us regain control, balance, and peace.

And so, this book is born from my deep desire to spread the healing potential that lies within our own bodies. In the pages that follow, I will guide you on a journey to understand the importance of the Vagus Nerve, its role in your overall health and well-being, and most importantly, how to nurture it. I will share practical exercises and advice, backed by science, that can help reduce anxiety, improve digestion, enhance sleep, and generally promote wellness.

My hope is that this book will illuminate your path to a deeper understanding of your body, to a more mindful and healthier way of living. Because, as I've discovered, when we listen to our bodies and honor their wisdom, we can truly thrive.

We'll embark on a journey to uncover the secrets of the Vagus nerve together, and by the end, you'll have the tools to boost your well-being and keep stress at bay. Let's get started on this adventure to a calmer, happier you!

CHAPTER 1

Anatomy and Functions of the Vagus Nerve

Why are we so intrigued by the human body? Perhaps it's because of its intricacy, its delicate balance, and its undoubted resilience. Or perhaps it's because every so often, we uncover a part of us that holds a key to our overall well-being. The Vagus Nerve, the longest cranial nerve in our body, is one such part. This nerve is not only fascinating because of its impressive reach within our bodies but also due to the profound influence it has on our overall health.

1.1 The Vagus Nerve: A Brief Overview

So, what is the Vagus Nerve exactly? Well, its name provides a hint. "Vagus" comes from the Latin word for "wandering," and indeed, this nerve wanders extensively throughout our bodies. Its journey begins in the brain, specifically in the medulla oblongata, part of the brainstem. From there, it ventures downwards, branching out in various directions to reach many of our vital organs such as the heart, lungs, and digestive tract.

As it takes its course, it makes connections with different parts of our bodies. Think of it as a network of communication lines, transmitting information between our brain and our organs. This intricate network allows the Vagus Nerve to perform a wide range of functions, from controlling muscle movements in our throat to regulating our heart rate and digestion.

The Vagus Nerve exhibits dual functionality, meaning it carries both sensory and motor information. In its sensory role, it collects information from our organs and sends it up to our brain. This information can include anything from the state of our gut microbiota to the rhythm of our heartbeats. On the flip side, as a motor nerve, it conveys instructions from our brain to our organs. These instructions can range from telling our heart to slow down when we are relaxed to signaling our stomach to start breaking down the food we've just eaten.

But the role of the Vagus Nerve extends beyond individual organ functions. It is a key player in our Autonomic Nervous System (ANS), the part of our nervous system that controls our bodily functions that occur without our conscious effort. The ANS is further divided into the Sympathetic Nervous System (SNS), which prepares our body for action, and the Parasympathetic Nervous System (PNS), which promotes relaxation and recovery. The Vagus Nerve is a significant part of the PNS, often termed the "rest and digest" system.

Picture a situation where you've just finished running a marathon. Your heart is pounding, your breathing is heavy, and your muscles are tense. This is your SNS in action, helping you cope with the physical demands of running. Now, imagine the moment you stop running. Your heart rate starts to slow down, your breathing becomes more relaxed, and your muscles begin to loosen. This transition to a relaxed state is largely due to the work of the Vagus Nerve and the PNS.

This ability of the Vagus Nerve to help our bodies transition from high-alert to a relaxed state has significant implications for our health. Over-activation of the SNS and under-activation of the PNS has been linked to chronic stress, anxiety, and various health issues.

So, understanding the Vagus Nerve isn't just a biological curiosity. Its functions, its connections, and its role in our bodies can impact our health in very real ways. By learning about the Vagus Nerve, we're not just adding to our knowledge of human anatomy. We're taking a step towards understanding how our bodies function, how we can keep them in balance, and how we can improve our health. This is the fundamental premise of this book and the journey we're on. As we delve further into the following chapters, we'll explore the Vagus Nerve in greater detail, understanding how it influences our health and how we can nurture it for overall wellness.

1.2 The Role of the Vagus Nerve in the Body

Regulating Heart Rate

Our heart rate isn't just a number that we check during our annual physicals or after a workout. It's a dynamic entity, constantly changing in response to what we're doing, feeling, or even thinking.

When we're faced with a stressful situation, our heart rate quickens, preparing us for action. On the other hand, when we're relaxed or sleeping, our heart rate slows down, conserving energy and allowing for restoration. This delicate balance between acceleration and deceleration is crucial for our overall well-being and, quite literally, life-sustaining.

Herein lies the significance of the Vagus Nerve. It plays a pivotal role in slowing down our heart rate. When we are at rest or in a state of relaxation, the Vagus Nerve sends signals to the heart, instructing it to slow down. These signals are carried to the heart's pacemaker cells, which control the rhythm of the heart. The pacemaker cells respond by reducing the rate at which they fire, leading to a slower heart rate.

Controlling Digestive Processes

Digestion, while often taken for granted, is a complex process involving multiple organs, enzymes, and a host of coordinated movements. The Vagus Nerve is intricately involved in this process, controlling and coordinating various aspects of digestion.

Consider the act of eating. As we chew and swallow food, the Vagus Nerve is at work, controlling the muscle movements in our throat to enable swallowing. Once the food reaches the stomach, the Vagus Nerve again plays a critical role by stimulating the release of stomach acid and digestive enzymes, facilitating the breakdown of food.

But the role of the Vagus Nerve doesn't stop at the stomach. It extends to the intestines, where it regulates the rhythmic contractions that propel the food along the digestive tract, a process known as peristalsis. It also controls the secretion of digestive enzymes in the intestines, which aid in the further breakdown and absorption of nutrients.

Facilitating Communication between Brain and Gut

In recent years, the connection between our brain and gut has gained considerable attention. Often referred to as the 'gut-brain axis', this bidirectional communication system allows our gut and brain to exchange information, influencing everything from our mood to our immune response.

Serving as a physical link in the gut-brain axis, the Vagus Nerve carries information from the gut to the brain and vice versa. On the one hand, it brings sensory information from the gut to the brain. This could be information about the type and quantity of nutrients in the gut, the activity of gut microbes, or any potential threats like inflammation or infection.

On the other hand, the Vagus Nerve also carries motor instructions from the brain to the gut. These could be instructions to increase or decrease the movement of the gut, to release digestive enzymes, or to modulate immune responses in the gut.

This crosstalk between the brain and gut, facilitated by the Vagus Nerve, is crucial for maintaining homeostasis and overall health. It allows our body to respond appropriately to changes in our internal and external environment, whether it's adjusting our digestion in response to a meal or modulating our immune response in the face of infection.

From regulating our heart rate and controlling digestion to facilitating crucial communication between our brain and gut, the Vagus Nerve is indeed a master regulator within our bodies. It underscores the interconnectedness of our body systems, reminding us that our health truly is a holistic endeavor. Understanding the functions of the Vagus Nerve allows us to appreciate the profound impact it has on our health and well-being.

1.3 The Connection between the Vagus Nerve and the Parasympathetic Nervous System

The Vagus Nerve's bond with the Parasympathetic Nervous System (PNS) is like a well-composed symphony. Each plays their part, creating a harmonious rhythm that keeps the body in a state of equilibrium. Let's explore this connection and its vital role in our health.

The PNS is the part of our Autonomic Nervous System that encourages relaxation and healing in our bodies, often described as the "rest and digest" response. It's the calming counterpart to the Sympathetic Nervous System (SNS), which triggers the "fight or flight" response when we're faced with stressful situations.

Imagine yourself in a serene garden, surrounded by blooming flowers and the gentle hum of nature. Your breathing slows, your heart rate decreases, and your muscles relax. This peaceful state is the work of the PNS, and the Vagus Nerve is at the heart of it.

Rest and Digest Response

The PNS, under the command of the Vagus Nerve, controls the "rest and digest" response. This response is activated when we're in a relaxed state, not facing any immediate threats or stressors. It's when our body shifts its resources towards maintenance and recovery tasks that often take a backseat during stressful situations.

For instance, when the "rest and digest" response is activated, our heart rate slows down, allowing for repair and recovery of the heart muscle. Our breathing becomes slow and deep, enhancing oxygen uptake and expelling toxins more effectively. The digestive system gets a boost, improving nutrient absorption and gut health.

Vagus Nerve as the Main Component

The Vagus Nerve is the primary conduit of the PNS, making it the main component of the "rest and digest" response. This nerve is like the conductor of the PNS orchestra, coordinating every section to create a harmonious performance.

The Vagus Nerve sends signals to various organs, instructing them to shift into "rest and digest" mode. This might mean signaling the heart to slow down, prompting the lungs to deepen the breath, or instructing the stomach to ramp up digestion.

But the role of the Vagus Nerve goes beyond sending signals. It also collects information from the body and conveys it back to the brain. This feedback mechanism allows the brain to adjust its instructions based on the body's needs, creating a finely tuned balance.

Impact on Body's Relaxation and Healing

The Vagus Nerve's role in the PNS and the "rest and digest" response has significant implications for our relaxation and healing. When we're in a state of constant stress or anxiety, the "fight or flight" response is overactive, and the "rest and digest" response is suppressed. This imbalance can lead to a host of health issues, from heart disease to digestive problems, and can interfere with our body's natural healing processes.

By contrast, when the Vagus Nerve is functioning well and the "rest and digest" response is activated, our body can focus on relaxation and healing. Our heart can recover from the strain of stress, our digestive system can efficiently process nutrients, and our immune system can effectively combat threats.

Moreover, the Vagus Nerve's role in relaxation extends to our mental well-being. It helps regulate our mood and anxiety levels, playing a critical role in mental health.

So, the Vagus Nerve is not just a nerve. It's a crucial part of our body's relaxation and healing mechanism. It's the conductor of the calming symphony that is the PNS. And by understanding its role and nurturing its function, we can enhance our body's ability to relax, heal, and thrive.

1.4 The Vagus Nerve and the Mind-Body Connection

A captivating facet of the Vagus Nerve is its role in the mind-body connection. This connection underscores the intricate interplay between our physical body and our mental and emotional state. The Vagus Nerve, with its extensive reach and diverse functions, is a dynamic player in this mind-body dialogue. Let's expand on this by examining its role in emotion regulation, its impact on social connection, and its influence on inflammation and immune response.

Role in Emotion Regulation

Emotions – those powerful feelings that paint our world in vivid colors. Joy, sadness, anger, fear, surprise, and disgust - these emotions frame our experiences and our reactions to the world around us. But have you ever wondered what manages these emotions within us? The answer, intriguingly, lies in part with the Vagus Nerve.

Research has shown that the Vagus Nerve is involved in regulating our emotional responses. When we experience different emotions, our body responds in various ways. Our heart rate may increase when we're excited, our stomach may churn when we're anxious, or our muscles may tense when we're angry. The Vagus Nerve, with its connections to the heart, digestive system, and muscles, plays a role in these physical responses.

Moreover, the Vagus Nerve also communicates these bodily responses to the brain. This feedback allows our brain to recognize and understand our emotional state. For instance, if our heart is racing and our muscles are tense, our brain may recognize this as a state of excitement or anxiety. This emotional awareness is crucial for appropriately responding to our environment and maintaining emotional balance.

Impact on Social Connection

Humans are inherently social creatures. We thrive on connection, understanding, and shared experiences. This ability to connect and communicate is not just about language or shared interests. It's also about being in tune with each other's feelings and emotional states. This emotional synchrony, as it's called, fosters empathy, understanding, and deep connection. And here again, the Vagus Nerve plays a pivotal role.

The Vagus Nerve is involved in subtle physical responses that facilitate social connection. For instance, it controls the muscles of our face and voice box, which we use for facial expressions and vocal intonation, crucial elements of non-verbal communication. Through these functions, the Vagus Nerve helps us express our emotions and understand the emotions of others, fostering empathy and connection.

Moreover, by regulating our heart rate and other bodily responses, the Vagus Nerve also influences how we physically respond to social interactions. For instance, when we empathize with someone, our heart rate may sync with theirs, a phenomenon facilitated by the Vagus Nerve. This synchronization can enhance our feelings of connection and understanding.

Influence on Inflammation and Immune Response

Inflammation - it's our body's first line of defense against injury or infection. However, when inflammation becomes chronic, it can lead to various health problems, from heart disease to autoimmune disorders. The Vagus Nerve, with its anti-inflammatory properties, plays a significant role in managing inflammation and thus our immune response.

The Vagus Nerve communicates with immune cells through a neurotransmitter called acetylcholine. Research has shown that acetylcholine can inhibit the production of pro-inflammatory molecules, thus reducing inflammation. By controlling the release of acetylcholine, the Vagus Nerve can influence our body's immune response and inflammation levels.

Moreover, through its sensory functions, the Vagus Nerve can detect increases in inflammation and convey this information to the brain. This feedback can prompt the brain to initiate anti-inflammatory responses, further managing inflammation levels.

Understanding and nurturing this function of the Vagus Nerve can be crucial in managing chronic inflammatory conditions.

In essence, the Vagus Nerve is a tangible link in the mind-body connection, bridging our physical, emotional, and social experiences. It reminds us that our health is not just about the physical body but also about our emotional well-being and our connection with others. And as we learn to nurture this nerve, we learn to nurture this connection, fostering a balanced and integrated approach to health.

CHAPTER 2

The Vagus Nerve and Anxiety: Unraveling the Connection

Picture a spider. Yes, you read that right, a spider. Now imagine it crawling up your arm. Did your heart skip a beat? Did you feel a chill run down your spine? Congratulations, you've just experienced a glimpse of your body's fight or flight response, a primitive survival mechanism that has been with us since our early days as cave-dwellers. Now, what if I told you that the Vagus Nerve plays a significant role in this response? Intriguing, isn't it? Let's explore this further.

2.1 The Science of Anxiety

Understanding Fight or Flight Response

Think about the last time you had a near miss while driving. Remember how time seemed to slow down?

How your senses sharpened, your heart pounded, and your palms went sweaty? That's your fight or flight response kicking in - a primal reaction that prepares your body to either confront or flee from a potential threat.

During this response, your body undergoes several changes. Your adrenal glands release adrenaline (also known as epinephrine), a hormone that increases your heart rate, blood pressure, and glucose levels, priming your body for action. Your senses become hyper-alert, and your muscles tense up, ready to spring into action.

Role of Vagus Nerve in Anxiety Response

The Vagus Nerve, as a key player in the Parasympathetic Nervous System (PNS), works like a calming counterpoint to this fight or flight response. While the Sympathetic Nervous System (SNS) gears your body up for action, the PNS, guided by the Vagus Nerve, helps your body to cool down and recover once the threat has passed.

When the Vagus Nerve gets the signal that the danger is over, it starts sending out messages to your body to switch off the fight or flight response. It tells your heart to slow down, your muscles to relax, and your senses to return to their normal state.

Here's a real-life example. Let's say you've just finished giving a nerve-wracking presentation. As you step off the stage, your heart is still racing, and your palms are sweaty - remnants of your fight or flight response. But as you sit down and start to relax, you'll notice your heart rate slowing down, your muscles loosening up - all thanks to the calming influence of your Vagus Nerve.

Impact of Chronic Stress on Vagus Nerve Function

While the fight or flight response is a normal and essential part of our survival mechanism, problems can arise when this response is continually activated due to chronic stress or anxiety. Over time, this can take a toll on your Vagus Nerve's ability to function optimally.

Chronic stress or anxiety keeps your body in a perpetual state of high alert, making it difficult for the Vagus Nerve to do its job of calming your body down. This can lead to a state of chronic 'underactivity' of the Vagus Nerve, a condition referred to as low vagal tone.

Low vagal tone has been associated with a myriad of health issues including cardiovascular conditions, inflammatory disorders, and yes, increased anxiety. This is because when the Vagus Nerve is underactive, it's less effective in managing your body's stress response, leading to heightened anxiety levels and lower resilience to stress.

To give you a clearer picture, imagine you're living in a noisy city where the relentless hustle and bustle keep your senses constantly stimulated. Over time, the continuous noise and activity can become overwhelming, making it difficult for you to relax, even in the comfort of your own home. This is akin to what happens in your body when chronic stress or anxiety prevents your Vagus Nerve from effectively calming your body down.

Understanding the science of anxiety and the role of the Vagus Nerve in managing our body's stress response is crucial in our quest for better health and well-being. It underscores the importance of nurturing our Vagus Nerve, not just for its direct roles in regulating our heart rate or aiding digestion, but also for its significant influence on our emotional health.

2.2 How the Vagus Nerve Influences Anxiety Levels

Vagus Nerve and Stress Hormones

Have you ever wondered how exactly your body knows when to release stress hormones? The secret lies in a delicate interplay between your brain, your nervous system, and your endocrine system. The Vagus Nerve, our focus of interest, plays a crucial role in this dance.

When faced with a stressful situation, your brain communicates this threat to your body via the nervous system. The Vagus Nerve, acting as a messenger, carries these signals from your brain to your adrenal glands, tiny organs located above your kidneys. On receiving these signals, your adrenal glands spring into action, releasing a surge of stress hormones, including adrenaline and cortisol.

These hormones trigger a cascade of physiological responses - your heart rate increases, your breathing speeds up, and your muscles tense up, preparing your body to either fight the threat or flee from it. This is your body's stress response in action, all orchestrated by the Vagus Nerve and the release of stress hormones.

Impact on Heart Rate Variability

Let's shift our attention to a critical indicator of stress and anxiety - heart rate variability (HRV). HRV refers to the variation in time between each heartbeat. While it might seem logical to assume that a steady, rhythmic heartbeat is a sign of good health, it's actually the opposite. A higher HRV, implying more variability between heartbeats, is typically a sign of good health and a well-functioning nervous system.

Now, where does the Vagus Nerve fit into this? The Vagus Nerve, being a major component of the parasympathetic nervous system, plays a significant role in regulating your heart rate. When you're relaxed, the Vagus Nerve sends signals to your heart to slow down, increasing the variability between heartbeats. However, during times of stress or anxiety, these signals are reduced, leading to a lower HRV.

Consequently, chronic stress or anxiety, which keeps your body in a constant state of high alert, can reduce your HRV, signaling an imbalance in your nervous system. By nurturing the Vagus Nerve and enhancing its function, we can improve our HRV, thus reducing anxiety levels and promoting overall wellbeing.

Role in Gut-Brain Communication

Moving on, let's discuss an exciting area of research that's rapidly gaining traction - the gut-brain axis. The gut-brain axis refers to the two-way communication between your gut and your brain. The Vagus Nerve, with its extensive network of nerve fibers, acts as the physical link in this axis, carrying messages back and forth between your gut and your brain.

Now, you might be wondering, how does this relate to anxiety? To answer this, we need to delve into the world of gut microbes. Our gut is home to trillions of microbes, collectively known as the gut microbiota. These microbes play a crucial role in our health, influencing everything from our immune system to our mood.

Research has shown that certain types of gut microbes can influence the production of neurotransmitters, chemical messengers that regulate our mood and emotions. These neurotransmitters, including serotonin and gamma-aminobutyric acid (GABA), are known to have a calming effect and can reduce anxiety.

The Vagus Nerve, acting as a communication channel, carries these mood-regulating signals from your gut to your brain. However, in situations of chronic stress or anxiety, this communication can get disrupted, leading to an imbalance in mood-regulating neurotransmitters and increased anxiety levels.

By stimulating the Vagus Nerve, we can enhance this gut-brain communication, helping to regulate our mood and reduce anxiety. Moreover, adopting a gut-friendly diet, rich in fiber and fermented foods, can support a healthy gut microbiota, further boosting this communication and promoting mental wellbeing.

As we unravel the connection between the Vagus Nerve and anxiety, we can clearly see how this single nerve influences our emotional health. Whether it's through regulating stress hormones, impacting our heart rate variability, or facilitating gut-brain communication, the Vagus Nerve plays a critical role in managing our stress response and anxiety levels. As we continue to explore this fascinating nerve, we'll discover how we can harness its potential to enhance our health and wellbeing.

2.3 The Vagus Nerve and Stress Response

Think of a time when you were startled by a sudden noise. Your heart rate probably spiked, your body tensed up, and you were on high alert. But once you realized there was no real threat, you likely started to calm down. This process of returning to a state of calm after a stressful situation is primarily driven by the Parasympathetic Nervous System (PNS), with the Vagus Nerve at the helm.

Activation of Parasympathetic Nervous System

The PNS is often described as the 'rest and digest' system. It works to counterbalance the effects of the Sympathetic Nervous System (SNS), which is responsible for the 'fight or flight' response during times of stress. When there's no longer a threat, the PNS, through the Vagus Nerve, sends signals throughout the body to promote relaxation and recovery.

One way the Vagus Nerve does this is by sending signals to the heart to slow down, reducing the heart rate. This is crucial because a high heart rate is one of the most immediate responses to stress. By slowing down the heart rate, the Vagus Nerve helps the body start the process of unwinding and returning to a state of calm.

Another critical function of the Vagus Nerve in activating the PNS is its role in controlling the breath. During stress, our breathing can become shallow and quick, which can perpetuate feelings of anxiety. The Vagus Nerve, however, encourages slow, deep breathing, which helps to calm the mind and body.

Role in Relaxation and Recovery

The Vagus Nerve doesn't just help with immediate relaxation following a stress response, it also plays a significant role in longer-term recovery. For instance, it helps regulate digestion, which often slows down during stress. By promoting digestive activity, the Vagus Nerve ensures that the body can effectively absorb nutrients, which are essential for recovery and overall health.

Sleep is another key area where the Vagus Nerve plays a role in recovery. Good quality sleep is crucial for the body to repair and restore itself, and the Vagus Nerve contributes to this by helping to regulate sleep patterns. It does this in part by promoting relaxation and reducing anxiety, both of which can contribute to better sleep.

Impact on Resilience and Stress Tolerance

Beyond its role in relaxation and recovery, the Vagus Nerve also plays a critical role in building resilience and stress tolerance. Resilience refers to our ability to bounce back from stressful situations, while stress tolerance is our ability to endure stress without adverse effects.

One of the ways the Vagus Nerve contributes to resilience is through its impact on our emotions. By regulating the heart rate and promoting relaxation, the Vagus Nerve helps to regulate our emotional response to stress. This can lead to more positive emotional reactions, even in the face of adversity, which is an essential aspect of resilience.

As for stress tolerance, the Vagus Nerve, through its influence on the PNS, helps to keep the stress response in check. It does this by ensuring that the body returns to a state of calm after a stressful event. Over time, this can lead to an increased ability to handle stress, enhancing stress tolerance.

In essence, the Vagus Nerve, through its influence on the PNS, plays a crucial role in managing the body's stress response. It not only helps the body return to a state of calm after stress but also plays a significant role in recovery and resilience. By understanding this, we can begin to appreciate the profound impact that the Vagus Nerve can have on our overall well-being. Through nurturing the Vagus Nerve, we can enhance our ability to handle stress and build resilience, paving the way towards better health and well-being.

2.4 Case Studies: The Vagus Nerve and Anxiety

Real-life Experiences of Anxiety Management

Let's take a moment to consider the story of Sarah, a 35-year-old woman who had been battling with chronic anxiety for several years. Countless sleepless nights, constant feelings of dread, and an inability to function optimally at work led Sarah to seek alternatives outside traditional therapy and medication. Upon learning about the Vagus Nerve and its potential to alleviate anxiety, Sarah began incorporating simple Vagus nerve stimulation exercises into her daily routine.

Over time, Sarah noticed profound changes. Her anxiety levels dropped, and she began to sleep better. She also reported feeling more resilient and capable of handling stress, highlighting the significant role the

Vagus Nerve played in her ability to manage anxiety more effectively.

Success Stories of Vagus Nerve Stimulation

Let's shift our attention to Mark, a 50-year-old man who had been suffering from severe anxiety for several decades. Traditional treatments, while somewhat effective, did not provide the relief Mark sought. Upon hearing about the potential benefits of Vagus Nerve stimulation, Mark decided to give it a try.

After several months of incorporating a variety of Vagus Nerve stimulation exercises into his routine, Mark reported a significant reduction in his anxiety levels. He also noticed an improvement in his digestion and sleep, further highlighting the far-reaching effects of Vagus Nerve stimulation on overall wellness. For Mark, Vagus Nerve stimulation was a game-changer, providing him with the tools to reclaim control over his life.

Scientific Studies on Vagus Nerve and Anxiety Reduction

The stories of Sarah and Mark are not stand-alone cases. Scientific studies have started to explore the potential benefits of Vagus Nerve stimulation on anxiety reduction. One such study published in the Journal of Psychiatric Research investigated the effects of transcutaneous Vagus Nerve Stimulation (tVNS) - a non-invasive form of Vagus Nerve stimulation - on patients with generalized anxiety disorder. The study found that after just a few weeks of tVNS treatment, participants reported a significant decrease in anxiety levels.

Another study, published in the journal Frontiers in Psychiatry, explored the benefits of yoga - a practice known to stimulate the Vagus Nerve - on anxiety reduction. The results were promising, with participants reporting reduced anxiety levels and improved mood after incorporating yoga into their routine.

These studies, along with the real-life experiences of individuals like Sarah and Mark, underscore the potential of Vagus Nerve stimulation as a natural and effective way to manage anxiety. However, it's important to remember that everyone's experience with anxiety is unique, and what works for one person may not work for another. Therefore, it's always advisable to seek professional advice when considering new treatment approaches.

As we sift through inspiring stories and scientific findings, the importance of the Vagus Nerve in managing anxiety becomes increasingly clear. It's a gentle reminder that our bodies possess an inherent wisdom, a built-in system designed to restore balance and promote well-being. By learning to tap into this wisdom, to stimulate and nurture our Vagus Nerve, we empower ourselves with a valuable tool for managing anxiety and enhancing our overall wellness.

As we move forward, we'll delve deeper into the world of the Vagus Nerve, exploring its potential to transform not just our mental health, but our physical health as well. We'll look at how the Vagus Nerve influences our digestion, our sleep, and even our immune system. The journey to wellness is an exciting one, full of insights, discoveries, and most importantly, hope. So, let's press on and continue to explore the remarkable powers of the Vagus Nerve.

CHAPTER 3

The Vagus Nerve and Digestive Health: A Road to Wellness

Have you ever wondered why you feel butterflies in your stomach when you're nervous? Or why your appetite decreases when you're stressed? To understand these phenomena, we need to explore a remarkable connection that exists within us - the gut-brain axis. This axis, a two-way communication system between our gut and our brain, plays a crucial role in our health, influencing everything from our mood to our immune response. At the heart of this communication superhighway is our much-talked-about Vagus Nerve. With this chapter, we will unravel the intricate relationship between the Vagus Nerve, our digestive system, and our overall well-being.

3.1 The Gut-Brain Axis: A Brief Introduction

Neurotransmitters

Imagine you are at a party, and you have just spotted a plate of your favorite cookies. As soon as you see them, you feel a surge of happiness. This emotion is not just a figment of your mind. It's a result of chemicals known as neurotransmitters at work in your brain. Neurotransmitters are the body's chemical messengers. They transmit signals across a synapse, the tiny gap between nerve cells, allowing various parts of the body to communicate with each other.

In the context of the gut-brain axis, neurotransmitters play a crucial role. For instance, serotonin, a neurotransmitter often called the 'feel-good hormone,' is mainly produced in the gut. Serotonin helps regulate mood, appetite, and sleep. It's no wonder then that a healthy gut is often associated with a positive mood!

Enteric Nervous System

Imagine a city with its own mayor, its own rules, and its own way of functioning, separate from the rest of the country. Sounds unusual, right? But there's a similar setup within your own body - your gut, or more specifically, your Enteric Nervous System (ENS). Often referred to as the 'second brain,' the ENS is a complex system of about 100 million neurons that governs the function of the gastrointestinal system.

The ENS works both independently and in conjunction with the brain in your head. It controls digestive processes like the transport of food and the secretion of digestive enzymes. It also communicates with the brain via the Vagus Nerve, sending it information about things like nutrient availability and gut health. This crosstalk between the ENS and the brain forms a significant part of the gut-brain axis.

Microbiota

Just as a garden thrives with a variety of plants and creatures, so does our gut thrive with a diverse array of microscopic organisms known as microbiota. This includes bacteria, viruses, and fungi. Our gut microbiota plays a key role in our overall health, affecting everything from digestion and nutrient absorption to immune function and inflammation.

In the context of the gut-brain axis, the gut microbiota can influence the production of neurotransmitters, thereby impacting our mood and mental health.

Certain types of gut bacteria, for example, are known to produce the majority of the body's serotonin.

Moreover, the gut microbiota can interact with the ENS, influencing gut motility and secretion. It also communicates with the brain via the Vagus Nerve, providing it with information about the state of the gut.

To sum up, the gut-brain axis, with its neurotransmitters, Enteric Nervous System, and microbiota, is a central player in our health. At the same time, the Vagus Nerve, serving as a two-way communication highway, enables and enhances this gut-brain dialogue. As we continue to explore this fascinating connection, we'll discover how nurturing the Vagus Nerve can promote digestive health, reduce anxiety, and enhance overall well-being.

3.2 The Role of the Vagus Nerve in Digestion

Gastric Motility

The journey of the food we consume is a fascinating process, a rhythmic dance propelled by a series of muscular contractions known as peristalsis. These waves of movement, starting from the esophagus and continuing down to the intestines, ensure the smooth passage of food through our digestive system. And who's the maestro orchestrating this dance? It's the Vagus Nerve.

Upon the consumption of food, the Vagus Nerve springs into action, sending signals to the muscles lining our digestive tract. These signals initiate a synchronized contraction and relaxation of these muscles, creating the wave-like movements required for peristalsis. This propulsion of food through the digestive tract is what we refer to as gastric motility.

However, the role of the Vagus Nerve isn't limited to merely initiating this process. It constantly monitors and adjusts the speed and intensity of these contractions, ensuring an optimal pace for digestion. It slows down the movement when we've consumed hard-to-digest food, allowing more time for breaking it down. Conversely, it speeds up the process when the food is easier to digest.

Nutrient Absorption

Once the food is broken down into its basic nutrients, the next step is to absorb these nutrients into our bloodstream. This absorption predominantly occurs in our small intestine, where tiny, finger-like projections called villi increase the surface area for absorption. Now, you might be wondering what role the Vagus Nerve plays in this process. It's not directly involved in the absorption of nutrients, but it sets the stage for it to happen efficiently.

The Vagus Nerve, through its influence on gastric motility, ensures that the food remains in the intestines for an optimal period. This allows sufficient time for the villi to absorb the maximum amount of nutrients. Additionally, the Vagus Nerve communicates with the brain about the type and quantity of nutrients absorbed. This feedback mechanism aids in regulating our appetite and maintaining our nutritional balance.

Gut Inflammation Regulation

Inflammation, the body's response to injury or infection, can be a friend or foe. It's beneficial when it helps fight off an infection or heal a wound. But when inflammation becomes chronic or occurs without a real threat, it can lead to various health issues. The gut is particularly susceptible to such inflammatory conditions, with disorders like Irritable Bowel Syndrome and Inflammatory Bowel Disease associated with chronic gut inflammation.

Here's where the Vagus Nerve steps in. Research has shown that the Vagus Nerve has anti-inflammatory properties. It communicates with immune cells in the gut, regulating their response to potential threats. In a healthy gut, the Vagus Nerve ensures a balanced immune response, preventing overreaction that can lead to inflammation.

Moreover, the Vagus Nerve can detect signs of inflammation in the gut and convey this information to the brain. This feedback allows the brain to initiate appropriate responses, such as changes in appetite or behavior, to mitigate the situation.

From regulating the rhythmic dance of digestion to setting the stage for nutrient absorption and keeping inflammation in check, the Vagus Nerve plays a pivotal role in our digestive health. By understanding these roles, we can appreciate the profound influence this single nerve has on our wellness. As we nurture our Vagus Nerve, we are, in essence, nurturing our gut, paving the way for better digestion, improved nutrient absorption, and overall health.

3.3 Nutrition for Vagus Nerve Health

Our bodies are akin to intricate, well-oiled machines, each part functioning in harmony with the other. The fuel for these machines? It's the food we consume, the nutrients we absorb. The Vagus Nerve, the star of our exploration, is no exception to this. It thrives on a diet rich in certain nutrients that enhance its function and promote its health. A closer look at these nutrients reveals three key players: probiotics, omega-3 fatty acids, and vitamins B and C.

Probiotic Foods

Probiotics, often referred to as 'good' or 'friendly' bacteria, are live microorganisms that provide health benefits when consumed in adequate amounts. They are found in a variety of foods, most notably fermented foods like yogurt, kefir, sauerkraut, and kimchi.

So, how do these microscopic allies aid the Vagus Nerve? The answer lies in their home - our gut. Once probiotics enter the gut, they can influence the gut microbiota, the community of microorganisms living in our intestines. This influence can alter the production of neurotransmitters, chemical messengers that communicate with the brain via the Vagus Nerve.

For example, certain types of probiotics can stimulate the production of the neurotransmitter serotonin, often referred to as the 'feel-good hormone.' Since the majority of serotonin is produced in the gut, an increase in its production can have significant implications for our mood and overall well-being.

Through their beneficial effects on the gut microbiota and neurotransmitter production, probiotics can enhance the function of the Vagus Nerve, thereby promoting digestive health and reducing anxiety.

Omega-3 Fatty Acids

Next up are omega-3 fatty acids, a type of fat that's often lauded for its heart health benefits. Foods rich in omega-3 fatty acids include fatty fish like salmon and mackerel, flaxseeds, chia seeds, and walnuts.

Omega-3 fatty acids, particularly one called docosahexaenoic acid (DHA), play a crucial role in brain health. DHA is a key component of the brain and is involved in the formation of nerve cells, including those of the Vagus Nerve.

By incorporating omega-3 rich foods into our diets, we can support the health of the Vagus Nerve and its ability to communicate effectively with the brain and the rest of the body.

Vitamin B and C Rich Foods

Last but not least, let's talk about vitamins, specifically vitamins B and C. These vitamins are found in a variety of foods, including whole grains, meats, fruits, and vegetables.

The B vitamins, including B6, B9 (folic acid), and B12, are essential for the health of our nervous system. They play a role in the production of neurotransmitters and the formation of the protective covering of nerve cells, known as the myelin sheath. An adequate intake of these vitamins can support the function of the Vagus Nerve, enhancing its ability to transmit signals effectively.

On the other hand, vitamin C, also known as ascorbic acid, plays a role in the production of collagen, a protein that provides structure to various tissues, including nerves. Vitamin C is also a potent antioxidant, protecting cells, including nerve cells, from damage caused by free radicals. Foods rich in vitamin C, such as citrus fruits, strawberries, bell peppers, and broccoli, can therefore support the health and function of the Vagus Nerve.

In the realm of nutrition, there's a saying that 'you are what you eat.' By choosing foods rich in probiotics, omega-3 fatty acids, and vitamins B and C, we can provide our Vagus Nerve with the nutrients it needs to function optimally. In doing so, we're not just nurturing this remarkable nerve; we're taking significant strides towards better digestion, reduced anxiety, and overall wellness.

3.4 Foods for an Optimal Vagus Nerve Function

Leafy Greens

A parade of vibrant colors, a medley of textures, and a burst of flavors - that's the magic of a bowl of fresh, leafy greens. Spinach, kale, Swiss chard, collard greens - they're not just a feast for the senses, but also a boon for our Vagus Nerve.

Packed with a variety of nutrients, leafy greens are particularly rich in dietary fiber. This fiber, while not digestible by our bodies, serves as a nourishing meal for our gut bacteria. These bacteria, in turn, ferment the fiber, producing short-chain fatty acids. These fatty acids can stimulate the Vagus Nerve, enhancing its function and promoting gut-brain communication.

Moreover, leafy greens are a good source of magnesium, a mineral that plays a role in nerve impulse conduction. A diet rich in leafy greens can therefore support the health and function of the Vagus Nerve.

Fatty Fish

The soft texture, the rich flavor, the satisfying savoriness - fatty fish, such as salmon, mackerel, and trout, are a delight for the palate. But beyond their culinary appeal, fatty fish are also a powerhouse of nutrients that can benefit the Vagus Nerve.

As discussed earlier, fatty fish are an excellent source of omega-3 fatty acids, particularly DHA. This fatty acid plays a crucial role in brain health, including the health of the Vagus Nerve. By including fatty fish in our diets, we can provide our Vagus Nerve with the nutrients it needs to function optimally.

Moreover, fatty fish are a good source of vitamin D, a nutrient that's been shown to promote nerve growth. So, by savoring a meal of grilled salmon or smoked mackerel, you're not just delighting your taste buds, but also nurturing your Vagus Nerve.

Fermented Foods

There's something uniquely satisfying about the tangy taste of fermented foods. Whether it's the fizzy bite of sauerkraut, the sour creaminess of yogurt, or the sharp savoriness of kimchi, fermented foods add a depth of flavor to our meals. But did you know that these foods also have profound benefits for the Vagus Nerve?

Fermented foods are rich in probiotics, the 'good' bacteria that can influence our gut microbiota. As we've explored earlier in this chapter, a healthy gut microbiota can enhance the function of the Vagus Nerve, promoting gut-brain communication and overall well-being.

Moreover, the process of fermentation can increase the availability of certain nutrients in foods, making them easier to absorb. This means that by consuming fermented foods, we can provide our Vagus Nerve with a plethora of nutrients that support its health and function.

Berries

Imagine biting into a ripe, juicy berry. The burst of sweetness, the slight tartness, the vibrant flavor - it's a sensory delight. But berries, with their array of colors and flavors, are not just a treat for the senses. They're also packed with nutrients that can benefit the Vagus Nerve.

Berries are a rich source of antioxidants, compounds that protect our cells, including nerve cells, from damage caused by harmful molecules called free radicals. They're also high in fiber, promoting gut health and consequently, the health of the Vagus Nerve.

Moreover, berries are a good source of vitamin C, a nutrient that's involved in the production of collagen, a protein that provides structure to various tissues, including nerves. By including a variety of berries in our diet, we can support the health and function of the Vagus Nerve.

As we explore the foods that can nurture our Vagus Nerve, we realize that nurturing this nerve is about more than just specific exercises or techniques. It's about embracing a lifestyle that supports overall health and well-being. It's about making choices that not only tantalize our taste buds but also nourish our bodies and minds.

So, the next time you sit down for a meal, remember that what's on your plate doesn't just satisfy your hunger. It also has the potential to influence your Vagus Nerve, your digestion, your mood, and so much more. With every bite, you're taking a step towards better health, reduced anxiety, and enhanced well-being.

As we peel back the layers of the Vagus Nerve and its influence on our health, we realize that this nerve is not just a part of our anatomy. It's a connection, a dialogue, a bridge between various aspects of our health. And as we continue to explore this fascinating nerve in the coming chapters, we'll discover how we can harness its potential to improve not just our digestive health, but also our sleep, our immune function, and our overall well-being. The path to wellness is an exciting one, full of insights, revelations, and most importantly, empowerment. So, let's press on and continue to uncover the remarkable potential of the Vagus Nerve.

CHAPTER 4

Embracing the Harmony of Sleep: The Role of Vagus Nerve

Imagine a symphony orchestra, each instrument playing its unique part, but all working together to create a harmonious melody. This is akin to how our bodies function. Various systems and processes, each with their unique roles, work cohesively, creating the symphony of life. Sleep, a seemingly passive state, is an integral part of this melody. It's a complex, active process involving various stages, each with its unique characteristics and functions. The conductor of this symphony? The Vagus Nerve, working diligently behind the scenes, guiding our bodies through the various stages of sleep and ensuring a restful night. Let's take a closer look at this intricate process.

4.1 Understanding the Sleep Cycle

REM Sleep

Often referred to as the dream stage of sleep, Rapid Eye Movement (REM) sleep is a unique phase of our sleep cycle. It's during REM sleep that our most vivid dreams occur. This stage is characterized by rapid movement of the eyes, increased brain activity, faster breathing, and temporary muscle paralysis.

The role of REM sleep extends beyond just being a stage for vivid dreams. It's considered crucial for memory consolidation, learning, and mood regulation. During REM sleep, our brain processes and stores information from the day, converting it from short-term to long-term memory.

Non-REM Sleep

Non-REM sleep, as the name suggests, is the stage of sleep when our eyes are not rapidly moving. It's further divided into three stages, each with its unique characteristics and functions.

- Stage 1: This is the lightest stage of sleep, a transition phase from wakefulness to sleep. During this stage, our heart rate and breathing slow down, and our muscles begin to relax.

- Stage 2: This is the first stage of true sleep. Our heart rate and breathing continue to slow down, our body temperature drops, and our muscles relax further.

- Stage 3: Often referred to as deep sleep or slow-wave sleep, this is the most restorative stage of sleep. It's during this stage that our body repairs and grows tissues, strengthens the immune system, and builds bone and muscle.

Circadian Rhythm

Each day, as the sun rises and sets, our bodies follow a natural rhythm or cycle, referred to as the circadian rhythm. This rhythm, controlled by a part of our brain called the hypothalamus, influences our sleep-wake cycle, feeding schedule, and various bodily functions like hormone production and cell regeneration.

Our circadian rhythm is primarily influenced by light and darkness. With the onset of darkness, our brain signals the production of melatonin, a hormone that promotes sleep. As light breaks, the production of melatonin decreases, signaling our bodies to wake up.

This natural rhythm is crucial for maintaining a healthy sleep cycle. Disruptions to this rhythm, like those caused by shift work or jet lag, can lead to sleep disorders and various health issues.

In this intricate dance of sleep stages and rhythms, the Vagus Nerve plays a vital role. Through its influence on our heart rate, breathing, and muscle relaxation, it guides our bodies through the various stages of sleep, ensuring a restful and restorative night's sleep. As we continue to explore the role of the Vagus Nerve in sleep, we'll learn how nurturing this nerve can enhance sleep quality, promote overall health, and improve our quality of life.

4.2 The Vagus Nerve and Sleep Quality

Sleep Apnea

Picture a calm lake, its surface smooth and undisturbed. Suddenly, a pebble is thrown into the water, creating ripples across the tranquil scene. The world of sleep can be likened to this peaceful lake, and disorders like sleep apnea are the disruptive pebbles. Sleep apnea is a condition characterized by pauses in breathing during sleep. These interruptions can range from a few seconds to minutes and happen multiple times per hour. This disorder is not just a thief of quality sleep but also a potential risk factor for several health issues, including heart disease, high blood pressure, and type 2 diabetes.

Now, where does the Vagus Nerve fit into this scenario? When functioning optimally, the Vagus Nerve controls the muscles that keep the airways open, allowing for smooth, uninterrupted breathing. However, in people with sleep apnea, the function of the Vagus Nerve may be compromised, leading to the collapse of the airway and subsequent pauses in breathing.

By enhancing the function of the Vagus Nerve through specific exercises and lifestyle modifications, we can improve the muscle control of our airways, potentially reducing the frequency and severity of sleep apnea episodes. This not only leads to better sleep quality but also decreases the risk of associated health complications.

Insomnia

Have you ever found yourself tossing and turning in bed, unable to drift off to the land of dreams? Or perhaps you've experienced nights where you wake up frequently, struggling to return to sleep. If these scenarios sound familiar, you've likely experienced the frustrating world of insomnia. Insomnia, a common sleep disorder, is characterized by difficulty falling asleep, staying asleep, or both, despite having an opportunity for adequate sleep.

The ripple effect of insomnia extends beyond just feeling tired or irritable. Chronic insomnia can lead to cognitive impairment, lowered immunity, and an increased risk of mental health disorders.

The Vagus Nerve, in its role as a pacifier of the body's stress response, can be a valuable ally in the battle against insomnia. When stimulated, the Vagus Nerve promotes relaxation and a sense of calm, both of which are conducive to falling asleep. Moreover, by regulating heart rate and breathing, the Vagus Nerve can help maintain a state of restful sleep, reducing the likelihood of frequent awakenings.

By prioritizing Vagus Nerve health, we can equip our bodies with a natural aid to combat insomnia, promoting restful nights and energetic days.

Restless Leg Syndrome

Imagine the urge to move your legs constantly, especially during periods of rest or inactivity. This irresistible urge often accompanied by uncomfortable sensations, is the hallmark of Restless Leg Syndrome (RLS), a neurological sensory disorder. RLS can be a significant disruptor of sleep, as the symptoms often worsen during the evening or night, making it difficult to fall asleep or maintain restful sleep.

Interestingly, the Vagus Nerve could have a role to play in managing RLS. As a key component of the parasympathetic nervous system, the Vagus Nerve helps regulate muscle relaxation. This function could potentially help alleviate the symptoms of RLS, reducing the urge to constantly move the legs.

Moreover, the Vagus Nerve can influence the production of neurotransmitters such as dopamine, which are thought to be involved in the pathology of RLS. By stimulating the Vagus Nerve, we can enhance the production of these neurotransmitters, potentially providing relief from the symptoms of RLS.

In the realm of sleep, the Vagus Nerve emerges as a versatile conductor, managing various aspects of sleep quality. Whether it's keeping the airways open for smooth breathing, promoting relaxation to combat insomnia, or regulating muscle relaxation to manage Restless Leg Syndrome, the Vagus Nerve plays a crucial role. By nurturing this valuable nerve, we can enhance our sleep quality, paving the path to restful nights and energetic mornings.

4.3 Simple Techniques for Better Sleep

Sleep Hygiene

Imagine a potter at work, molding clay into a beautiful vase. The right techniques and careful attention to detail turn a lump of clay into an exquisite piece of art. The same principle applies to our sleep. Just as a potter needs the right skills and tools to create a vase, we need the right habits and routines to cultivate restful sleep. This is the essence of sleep hygiene, a set of practices that can set the stage for better sleep.

One of the most impactful sleep hygiene practices is maintaining a consistent sleep schedule. Going to bed and waking up at the same time each day, even on weekends, can help regulate our body's internal clock, making it easier to fall asleep and wake up.

Another key element of sleep hygiene is being mindful of what we consume. Caffeine and alcohol, especially close to bedtime, can interfere with our sleep cycle. Similarly, heavy, rich meals late in the night can cause discomfort and disrupt our sleep.

Lastly, incorporating regular physical activity into our daily routine can promote better sleep. Exercise, especially aerobic activities like walking or cycling, can help us fall asleep faster and enjoy deeper sleep.

Sleep Environment Optimization

Now, let's turn our attention to the space where sleep unfolds - our bedroom. Just as a gardener carefully prepares the soil before planting seeds, we need to create a conducive sleep environment to cultivate restful sleep.

A crucial aspect of this environment is comfort. A good quality mattress that supports our body and pillows that maintain the natural alignment of our neck can make a significant difference. The right bedding, which feels soft against our skin and keeps us at a comfortable temperature, can also enhance our sleep experience.

Next, we need to consider light and noise, two factors that can significantly impact our sleep. Using heavy curtains or an eye mask can block out light, and earplugs or a white noise machine can help drown out disruptive sounds.

Lastly, keeping our bedroom tidy and free from clutter can create a sense of tranquility, making it easier to relax and fall asleep.

Bedtime Routine

As the sun sets, a cue for the day to wind down, our bodies too need signals to prepare for sleep. A bedtime routine, a series of relaxing activities before sleep, serves as these signals, cueing our body and mind to wind down.

A warm bath or shower can be a great start to our bedtime routine. The rise and subsequent fall in body temperature can promote feelings of drowsiness.

Next, we could include a relaxation technique, such as deep breathing, progressive muscle relaxation, or meditation. These techniques can help quiet our mind and relax our body, preparing us for sleep.

Lastly, engaging in a calming activity, like reading a book or listening to soft music, can further enhance our relaxation. However, it's best to avoid screens during this time, as the blue light they emit can interfere with our sleep.

By nurturing the Vagus Nerve through these simple yet effective techniques, we can cultivate better sleep, paving the way for restful nights and energized mornings. As this remarkable nerve continues to guide us through the realms of sleep and relaxation, we uncover its profound potential to enhance our overall well-being.

4.4 The Impact of Sleep on Vagus Nerve Function

Stress Response

Imagine the ebb and flow of waves on a shoreline. This rhythmic pattern, a calming spectacle of nature, mirrors the way our bodies respond to stress, alternating between phases of high alert and relaxation. The orchestrator of this rhythm? The Vagus Nerve, a master regulator that helps our bodies navigate the undulating seas of stress.

During deep, restorative sleep, our bodies switch to a state of relaxation and recovery, a stage where the Vagus Nerve takes center stage. It sends signals to our organs to slow down and recover from the day's stress. Our heart rate slows, our breathing becomes deeper, and our muscles relax - all under the Vagus Nerve's watchful guidance.

Just as a well-rested athlete performs better, a well-rested Vagus Nerve functions more efficiently. Adequate sleep allows the Vagus Nerve to recover from the day's activity, preparing it for the next wave of stress. This recovery enhances the Vagus Nerve's ability to manage our body's stress response, helping us maintain a state of calm amidst life's storms.

Immune System Function

Our immune system, our body's defense mechanism, is a silent warrior that tirelessly protects us from harmful invaders. However, this warrior needs rest to function optimally, and sleep is its preferred form of rest. During sleep, our immune system goes into overdrive, producing proteins called cytokines that help fight infections and inflammation.

The Vagus Nerve, in its role as a messenger, communicates with our immune cells, regulating their response to threats. During deep sleep, when our bodies are relaxed, the Vagus Nerve's signals to the immune system are more effective, enhancing our body's defense mechanism.

Moreover, the Vagus Nerve can detect signs of infection or inflammation and convey this information to the brain. This feedback allows the brain to initiate appropriate immune responses, further strengthening our body's defenses. By prioritizing sleep, we not only promote the health of our immune system but also enhance the function of our Vagus Nerve, creating a powerful duo for optimal health.

Cognitive Function

Have you ever noticed how a good night's sleep clears your mind, making you more alert and focused? This isn't just a perception. During sleep, our brain goes through a process of consolidation, where it processes and stores information from the day. This process is crucial for learning, memory, and overall cognitive function.

The Vagus Nerve, with its extensive connections to the brain, plays a role in this process. It communicates with various areas of the brain, facilitating the transfer of information. During deep sleep, this communication becomes more effective, enhancing the process of memory consolidation and learning.

Moreover, the Vagus Nerve influences the production of neurotransmitters like acetylcholine, which are crucial for attention and memory. Adequate sleep can enhance the production of these neurotransmitters, improving cognitive function and mental clarity.

In essence, sleep isn't just a time of rest for our bodies; it's also a time of restoration and rejuvenation for our Vagus Nerve. By prioritizing sleep, we enhance the function of our Vagus Nerve, enabling it to manage stress more effectively, boost our immune function, and improve cognitive performance. As we foster a healthy relationship with sleep and our Vagus Nerve, we equip ourselves with the tools for a balanced, resilient, and vibrant life.

As we close this chapter, let us remember that nurturing our Vagus Nerve requires a comprehensive, holistic approach, one that includes not just specific exercises or techniques but also lifestyle choices like our diet and sleep habits. Each choice we make, each step we take towards nurturing our Vagus Nerve, is a step towards better health, reduced anxiety, and improved well-being. As we move forward, we'll continue to explore the remarkable potential of the Vagus Nerve and learn how we can harness its power to transform our health and our lives.

CHAPTER 5

The Vagus Nerve: A Key to Unlocking Autoimmune Wellness

Imagine a bustling city, its streets filled with a constant ebb and flow of traffic. The city's traffic control system, a network of traffic lights and signs, ensures a smooth flow of vehicles, preventing accidents and chaos. Now, consider your body as this city, and the Vagus Nerve as its traffic control system. Just as traffic lights control the speed and direction of vehicles, the Vagus Nerve regulates various bodily functions, maintaining balance and preventing disorders. This chapter aims to shed light on the connection between the Vagus Nerve and autoimmune diseases, and how nurturing this connection can unlock the path to wellness.

5.1 The Vagus Nerve and Autoimmune Diseases

Autoimmune diseases are like a case of mistaken identity. In these conditions, our immune system, the body's defender against harmful invaders, mistakenly attacks our own cells, causing inflammation and damage. Here, we'll explore three such conditions - Rheumatoid Arthritis, Multiple Sclerosis, and Lupus - and the role of the Vagus Nerve in these diseases.

Rheumatoid Arthritis

Imagine waking up to a sunrise, ready to embrace the day, but your body feels stiff, your joints painful and swollen. This is a reality for those suffering from Rheumatoid Arthritis (RA), a chronic autoimmune condition characterized by inflammation in the joints.

So, where does the Vagus Nerve fit into this picture? One of its roles is to regulate inflammation. Studies have shown that stimulation of the Vagus Nerve can reduce the production of pro-inflammatory cytokines, proteins that promote inflammation in the body. By dampening this inflammatory response, the Vagus Nerve can potentially alleviate the symptoms of RA, improving joint mobility and reducing pain.

Multiple Sclerosis

Picture a well-insulated electrical wire, efficiently conducting electrical signals. Now imagine if the insulation was damaged, causing the signals to slow down or get lost. This is similar to what happens in Multiple Sclerosis (MS), a condition where the immune system attacks the protective covering of nerve fibers, disrupting the communication between the brain and the rest of the body.

The Vagus Nerve, which runs from the brain to various organs in the body, can also be affected in MS. Research suggests that Vagus Nerve stimulation can enhance neuroplasticity, the brain's ability to form and reorganize synaptic connections, especially in response to learning or experience or following injury. This could potentially improve the symptoms of MS, enhancing communication between the brain and the body.

Lupus

In a world full of diverse faces, our body's immune system is like a skilled artist, able to recognize and remember a myriad of faces, distinguishing friend from foe. But in Lupus, this recognition system falters, and the immune system starts attacking the body's own cells.

The Vagus Nerve, with its anti-inflammatory properties, can play a significant role in managing Lupus. Research has shown that Vagus Nerve stimulation can reduce the production of antibodies, proteins produced by the immune system that mistakenly attack the body's own cells in Lupus. This can help manage the symptoms of Lupus, reducing inflammation, and promoting overall wellness.

Vagus Nerve Stimulation: A Practical Approach

Understanding the connection between the Vagus Nerve and autoimmune diseases is just the first step. The next step is to incorporate practical strategies to stimulate the Vagus Nerve, thereby managing these conditions.

Here are some simple yet effective strategies:

- **Deep Breathing Techniques**: Practices such as diaphragmatic breathing and box breathing can stimulate the Vagus Nerve, promoting relaxation and reducing inflammation.

- **Yoga and Meditation**: These mind-body practices can enhance Vagus Nerve function, improve stress resilience, and promote a sense of calm.

- **Cold Exposure**: Brief exposure to cold, such as a cold shower or face dunking, can activate the Vagus Nerve, enhancing its function.

- **Singing or Humming**: These activities can stimulate the Vagus Nerve, as it is connected to the vocal cords and the muscles of the throat.

- **Probiotic-Rich Diet**: Consuming foods rich in probiotics can improve gut health, which in turn can enhance Vagus Nerve function.

Implementing these strategies can be like watering a plant, nurturing the root (Vagus Nerve) to ensure the plant (our body) thrives. By taking these steps, we can harness the potential of the Vagus Nerve to manage autoimmune diseases and pave the path to wellness.

5.2 The Vagus Nerve and Heart Health

Picture your heart as a metronome, ticking away in a steady rhythm that sets the pace for your body's symphony. This rhythm, while seemingly constant, subtly varies with every beat, creating a unique pattern known as Heart Rate Variability (HRV). This pattern, much like the conductor of an orchestra, is controlled by the Vagus Nerve. Together, they play a crucial role in maintaining the harmony of our heart's function and our overall health.

Heart Rate Variability

HRV is the physiological phenomenon of variation in the time interval between consecutive heartbeats. Contrary to what one might assume, a healthy heart does not tick away like clockwork, with uniform intervals between each beat. Instead, there is a constant, subtle variation in these intervals, creating a pattern that is unique to each individual.

The Vagus Nerve, a key component of the parasympathetic nervous system, is the primary regulator of HRV. When the Vagus Nerve sends signals to the heart, it slows down the heart rate, leading to increased variability between heartbeats. Conversely, under stress or during physical activity, when the influence of the Vagus Nerve is reduced, the heart rate speeds up, and the variability decreases.

HRV is considered a robust indicator of heart health and overall well-being. Higher HRV, signifying a more responsive and resilient heart, is associated with good cardiovascular health, stress resilience, and even emotional well-being. By nurturing the Vagus Nerve, we can enhance our HRV, paving the way for a healthier heart and a healthier life.

Blood Pressure Regulation

From the towering mountains to the vast oceans, pressure is a fundamental force that shapes our world. In our bodies, blood pressure, the force exerted by blood against the walls of our blood vessels, is a vital sign of our health. Just as the earth's pressure systems maintain the balance of our planet's climate, our body's pressure system, regulated in part by the Vagus Nerve, maintains the balance of our health.

The Vagus Nerve, through its influence on the heart and blood vessels, plays a crucial role in regulating blood pressure. When activated, it causes the heart rate to slow down and the blood vessels to relax, leading to a decrease in blood pressure. This function of the Vagus Nerve is particularly important in managing our body's response to stress. During stress, our blood pressure tends to rise, preparing our body for 'fight or flight.' However, once the stressor is removed, it's essential for our blood pressure to return to normal to prevent undue strain on our heart and blood vessels. Here, the Vagus Nerve steps in, calming the heart and relaxing the blood vessels, bringing the blood pressure back to baseline.

By understanding and nurturing the role of the Vagus Nerve in blood pressure regulation, we can support our cardiovascular health and reduce the risk of conditions like hypertension, heart disease, and stroke.

Arrhythmia Prevention

Let's think of our heart's rhythm again, this time as a dance. In a perfectly choreographed dance, each step follows the next in a predictable pattern, creating a beautiful performance. However, if the dancers are out of sync, the performance can quickly become chaotic. The same principle applies to our heart. If the heart's rhythm becomes irregular, it can lead to conditions known as arrhythmias, which can be potentially life-threatening.

The Vagus Nerve, the maestro of our heart's rhythm, plays a crucial role in preventing arrhythmias. It does this by maintaining a balance between the sympathetic nervous system, which speeds up the heart rate, and the parasympathetic nervous system, which slows it down.

During times of stress or physical activity, when the heart rate speeds up, the Vagus Nerve ensures that this acceleration does not go unchecked. It sends signals to the heart to slow down, preventing excessively rapid heart rates that can lead to arrhythmias. On the other hand, during periods of rest, when the heart rate slows down, the Vagus Nerve ensures that it does not slow down too much, preventing excessively slow heart rates that can also lead to arrhythmias.

By nurturing the Vagus Nerve and its role in regulating heart rhythm, we can help keep our heart dancing to the right beat, reducing the risk of arrhythmias and promoting overall heart health.

In our exploration of the Vagus Nerve and heart health, we've discovered the profound influence this single nerve has on our heart's rhythm, our blood pressure, and our risk of arrhythmias. But what's truly fascinating is that this influence extends beyond our heart to our overall health and well-being. By nurturing our Vagus Nerve, we are, in essence, nurturing our heart, and by nurturing our heart, we are nurturing our health, our life, and our future.

5.3 The Impact of Chronic Pain on the Vagus Nerve

Fibromyalgia

Fibromyalgia, a chronic pain disorder, is like a haunting melody. It lingers in the background of an individual's life, its persistent tune causing widespread discomfort and fatigue. While the exact cause of fibromyalgia remains unknown, one common thread is a heightened sensitivity to pain.

The Vagus Nerve, our body's information superhighway, carries pain signals from the body to the brain. In fibromyalgia, these signals may get amplified, resulting in an increased perception of pain. However, the Vagus Nerve also has the potential to be part of the solution. By stimulating the Vagus Nerve, we can influence how pain signals are processed, potentially reducing the intensity of the perceived pain. This stimulation can also help activate the body's natural pain-relief mechanisms, further alleviating discomfort.

Migraines

Consider the agony of a migraine; it's not just a headache. It's a throbbing pain, often accompanied by nausea, vomiting, and sensitivity to light and sound. The misery of a migraine attack can last for hours, sometimes even days, making it a significant source of chronic pain for many individuals.

In the context of migraines, the Vagus Nerve again surfaces as a critical player. Recent research suggests that an overactive Vagus Nerve might contribute to the development of migraines by facilitating a wave of electrical activity in the brain known as cortical spreading depression. This wave of activity is thought to trigger the intense pain of a migraine.

On the flip side, stimulating the Vagus Nerve has been shown to help reduce the frequency and severity of migraines. This stimulation can influence the production of neurotransmitters like serotonin, which play a role in pain regulation, providing some relief from the debilitating pain of migraines.

Chronic Back Pain

Imagine carrying a heavy backpack all day, every day. The constant strain, the relentless pressure – that's what chronic back pain feels like to those who experience it. It's a persistent discomfort that can dramatically impact quality of life.

The Vagus Nerve, in its capacity as a pain regulator, is relevant to the conversation about chronic back pain. The nerve carries pain signals from various parts of the body, including the back, to the brain. In situations of chronic pain, these signals may become intensified or continuous, leading to a heightened perception of pain.

However, the Vagus Nerve is also a conduit for the body's natural pain-relief mechanisms. By stimulating the Vagus Nerve, we can boost these mechanisms, potentially reducing the intensity of chronic back pain. Furthermore, Vagus Nerve stimulation can promote relaxation and reduce tension in the muscles, which can further alleviate back pain.

In the realm of chronic pain, the Vagus Nerve emerges as a key player. By transmitting pain signals and activating the body's natural pain-relief mechanisms, it plays a dual role – a carrier of discomfort but also a potential pathway to relief. By understanding and nurturing the Vagus Nerve, we can influence our body's pain response and potentially alleviate the burden of chronic pain conditions like fibromyalgia, migraines, and chronic back pain. Though the melody of chronic pain may be persistent, the Vagus Nerve holds the potential to change its tune, creating a symphony of relief and comfort.

5.4 The Vagus Nerve and Respiratory Health

Asthma

Picture a beautiful spring day, the air filled with the sweet scent of blossoming flowers. But for individuals with asthma, this idyllic scene could trigger an onslaught of symptoms including wheezing, chest tightness, shortness of breath, and coughing. Asthma, a chronic condition that inflames and narrows the airways, can turn the simple act of breathing into a struggle.

The Vagus Nerve, with its extensive reach, innervates the airways. When functioning optimally, it helps regulate the muscles that keep the airways open, allowing for smooth, unobstructed breathing. However, in individuals with asthma, the function of the Vagus Nerve may be compromised, leading to constriction of the airways and subsequent breathing difficulties.

But the Vagus Nerve also has the potential to be part of the solution. By stimulating the Vagus Nerve, we can enhance its function, potentially improving the muscle control of our airways and reducing the frequency and severity of asthma attacks.

Chronic Obstructive Pulmonary Disease

Consider a narrow, winding path, its route filled with obstacles making it difficult to traverse. This is akin to what happens in Chronic Obstructive Pulmonary Disease (COPD), a group of lung diseases characterized by breathlessness due to obstructed airflow from the lungs.

The Vagus Nerve, in its capacity as a regulator of the respiratory system, is relevant to the conversation about COPD. It controls the muscles of the airways, ensuring they remain open for unobstructed airflow. In COPD, where the airways are persistently blocked or narrowed, enhancing the function of the Vagus Nerve could potentially improve airflow, reduce breathlessness, and enhance overall respiratory health.

Cystic Fibrosis

Imagine a riverbed, its water flowing freely. Now imagine if the riverbed was clogged with debris, disrupting the free flow of water. This scenario mirrors what happens in Cystic Fibrosis (CF), a genetic disorder that causes persistent lung infections and limits the ability to breathe over time.

In CF, a defect in the CFTR gene leads to the production of thick, sticky mucus in various organs, including the lungs. This mucus can clog the airways, leading to breathing difficulties and persistent lung infections.

The Vagus Nerve, with its influence on the respiratory system, can play a role in managing the symptoms of CF. Vagus Nerve stimulation has been shown to reduce inflammation, a common occurrence in CF due to persistent infections. This can potentially alleviate some of the symptoms of CF, improving respiratory function and enhancing the quality of life for individuals with this condition.

Pulmonary Hypertension

Imagine a high-altitude mountain climb, the thin air making each breath a struggle. This is analogous to what individuals with Pulmonary Hypertension (PH) experience. PH is a type of high blood pressure that affects the arteries in the lungs and the right side of the heart, making it harder to breathe.

The Vagus Nerve, in its role as a key player in the cardiovascular and respiratory systems, has implications for PH. It regulates heart rate and blood vessel constriction, two factors that are often altered in PH. By enhancing Vagus Nerve function, we may be able to manage these factors, potentially improving symptoms and enhancing the quality of life for individuals with PH.

In each breath we take, in each beat of our hearts, the Vagus Nerve is there, guiding, regulating, balancing. Its influence extends from autoimmune diseases to heart health, from pain management to respiratory health. As we nurture this remarkable nerve, we unlock the potential to manage various health conditions, paving the path to wellness. And as we move forward, we continue to discover the vast potential of the Vagus Nerve, an exploration that empowers us to transform our health and our lives.

CHAPTER 6

Engaging the Power of Breath: Vagus Nerve Stimulation Exercises

Visualize a calm lake, its surface smooth and unruffled. Now imagine a pebble dropping into the lake, creating ripples that spread across the surface. The breath, much like that pebble, can create ripples of change within us, especially when it comes to activating the Vagus Nerve. Our breath, indeed, is a powerful, accessible, and effective tool for stimulating the Vagus Nerve, promoting relaxation, and reducing anxiety.

As you read this chapter, I invite you to think of your breath as a bridge, a connection between your mind and your body. It's a bridge we can cross at any time, a bridge that can lead us to a place of calm and balance. In this chapter, we'll explore three deep breathing techniques that can help you cross this bridge and stimulate your Vagus Nerve.

6.1 Deep Breathing Exercises

Box Breathing

Box breathing, also known as four-square breathing, is a simple yet powerful breathing technique that can stimulate the Vagus Nerve and promote relaxation. As the name suggests, box breathing involves four equal parts, much like the four equal sides of a box.

To practice box breathing:

1. Find a quiet, comfortable place to sit or lie down. Close your eyes and take a few normal breaths to settle in.

2. Slowly exhale all the air from your lungs.

3. Inhale slowly through your nose for a count of four.

4. Hold your breath for a count of four.

5. Slowly exhale through your mouth for a count of four.

6. Hold the breath again for a count of four.

7. Repeat this cycle for a few minutes, or as long as it feels comfortable.

As you practice this technique, visualize each side of the box being drawn as you complete each step. This can help focus your mind and enhance the relaxation effect.

4-7-8 Breathing

The 4-7-8 breathing technique, often referred to as "relaxing breath," involves inhaling for 4 seconds, holding the breath for 7 seconds, and exhaling for 8 seconds. This technique is particularly effective for calming the mind and can be a great way to prepare for sleep.

To practice 4-7-8 breathing:

1. Find a comfortable place to sit or lie down. Close your eyes and take a few normal breaths.

2. Inhale quietly through your nose for a count of four.

3. Hold your breath for a count of seven.

4. Exhale slowly through your mouth for a count of eight, making a gentle "whoosh" sound.

5. This completes one breath cycle. Repeat this cycle for four full breaths.

As you practice this technique, focus on the counting to help clear your mind and stimulate the Vagus Nerve.

Diaphragmatic Breathing

Diaphragmatic breathing, also known as belly breathing or deep breathing, is a technique that encourages full oxygen exchange in the body. It's beneficial for slowing the heartbeat, lowering blood pressure, and stimulating the Vagus Nerve.

To practice diaphragmatic breathing:

1. Lie down on your back on a flat surface or in bed. Bend your knees and keep your head supported.

2. Place one hand on your upper chest and the other on your belly, just below your rib cage.

3. Take a slow, deep breath in through your nose, allowing your belly to push your hand out. Your chest should remain still.

4. Exhale slowly through pursed lips, noticing your belly fall under your hand.

5. Continue these slow, deep breaths, focusing on the rise and fall of your belly.

As you practice these breathing techniques, remember that the goal is not perfection. It's about exploring the power of your breath, about crossing that bridge between your mind and body. It's about tuning into the rhythm of your breath and noticing the ripples of calm spreading across your body. As you harness the power of your breath, you stimulate your Vagus Nerve, stepping into a space of calm and balance, and paving the way for greater health and wellness.

6.2 Gentle Yoga Poses for Vagus Nerve Health

Child's Pose

Picture a serene garden, the scent of blossoming flowers filling the air and a gentle breeze rustling the leaves. A sense of calm washes over you as you sit down on the soft grass, your body naturally folding into a comfortable position. This tranquility, this sense of being grounded, is what the Child's Pose in yoga encapsulates.

To practice the Child's Pose:

1. Begin by kneeling on the floor, your big toes touching each other. Sit back on your heels and spread your knees hip-width apart.

2. As you exhale, bend forward, draping your torso between your thighs. Allow your forehead to rest on the floor.

3. Extend your arms in front of you, palms facing down. Alternatively, you can rest your arms along your body, palms facing up.

4. Stay in this pose for a few breaths, allowing your body to relax and sink deeper into the pose with each exhale.

Child's Pose is a restorative posture that promotes relaxation and stress relief. It gently stretches the hips, thighs, and ankles while calming the brain, making it therapeutic for relieving stress and anxiety. As you surrender to the pose, you stimulate the Vagus Nerve, encouraging a sense of calm and balance to ripple through your body.

Legs-Up-The-Wall Pose

Visualize a quiet beach, the rhythmic sound of waves lapping against the shore lulling you into a state of relaxation. You lie down on the warm sand, your legs propped up against a wall of sand, and a sense of ease envelops you. This is the essence of the Legs-Up-The-Wall Pose in yoga, an inversion pose that promotes relaxation and rejuvenation.

To practice the Legs-Up-The-Wall Pose:

1. Begin by sitting sideways against a wall.

2. As you exhale, gently swing your legs up onto the wall as you pivot your body to lie down on your back. Your body should form a 90-degree angle with the wall.

3. Rest your arms by your sides, palms facing up.

4. Close your eyes and take slow, deep breaths, allowing your body to relax completely.

The Legs-Up-The-Wall Pose is particularly beneficial for relieving tired legs and feet. It also helps to quiet the mind and can be very calming for the nervous system, making it an excellent pose for stimulating the Vagus Nerve and reducing anxiety and stress.

Savasana

Imagine lying on a cloud, your body weightless and your mind free from all worries. This sense of complete relaxation and surrender is what Savasana, also known as the Corpse Pose, aims to achieve.

To practice Savasana:

1. Lie down on your back. Extend your legs and allow them to fall open naturally. Relax your arms by your sides, palms facing up.

2. Close your eyes and take a few moments to settle into the pose. Allow your body to feel heavy against the floor.

3. Bring your awareness to your breath. Don't try to control it; just observe the natural rhythm of your inhales and exhales.

4. Allow any thoughts or worries to float away with each exhale.

Savasana is the ultimate pose for relaxation and stress relief. It encourages deep rest and recovery, making it extremely beneficial for Vagus Nerve stimulation. As you melt into the pose, you allow the Vagus Nerve to work its magic, guiding your body into a state of deep relaxation and peace.

These gentle yoga poses, with their focus on relaxation and mindful breathing, can effectively stimulate the Vagus Nerve, promoting a sense of calm and well-being. As you practice these poses, remember to listen to your body, respecting its limits and capabilities. Whether you're a seasoned yogi or a beginner, these poses can be a great addition to your wellness toolkit, helping you foster a healthy relationship with your Vagus Nerve and navigate the path to holistic health.

6.3 Relaxation Techniques for Vagus Nerve Stimulation

Progressive Muscle Relaxation

Imagine a tightly wound spring; each coil presses against the other, creating tension and resistance. Now envision that spring gently unravelling, each coil releasing its grip, leading to a state of relaxation. This is the essence of Progressive Muscle Relaxation (PMR), a technique that involves tensing and then releasing various muscle groups to promote relaxation.

To practice PMR:

1. Begin by finding a quiet, comfortable place to sit or lie down. Close your eyes and take a few deep breaths.

2. Start with your feet. Tense the muscles as much as you can and hold for about five seconds.

3. Relax the muscles in your feet and take a few deep breaths.

4. Move up to your calves and repeat the process. Continue to do this for all the muscle groups in your body, working your way up to your head.

5. Once you've completed the entire body, take a few moments to enjoy the feeling of relaxation.

PMR is not just about the physical release of tension; it's also a form of mindfulness. It brings your attention to the present moment and to your physical body, effectively engaging the Vagus Nerve and promoting a sense of calm and relaxation.

Guided Imagery

Picture a serene forest, the air crisp and fresh, the leaves rustling gently in the breeze. This image, vivid and calming, can transport you to a place of peace and relaxation. This is the power of Guided Imagery, a technique that uses visualizations to promote relaxation and reduce stress.

To practice Guided Imagery:

1. Find a quiet place where you won't be disturbed. Sit or lie down in a comfortable position.

2. Close your eyes and take a few deep breaths to help you relax.

3. Imagine a peaceful place or situation. Try to use all your senses – what do you see, hear, smell, and feel in this relaxing place?

4. Stay in this peaceful place for a few minutes, allowing the relaxation to seep into every part of your body.

Guided Imagery works by engaging the Vagus Nerve and activating the relaxation response in your body. It's like taking a mini-vacation in your mind, providing a much-needed break from stress and anxiety.

Autogenic Training

Think of a warm, cozy blanket wrapping around you, its softness enveloping you in a cocoon of comfort and relaxation. This sense of warmth and heaviness is what Autogenic Training aims to create. Autogenic

Training is a relaxation technique that uses both visual imagery and body awareness to reduce stress.

To practice Autogenic Training:

1. Find a quiet place where you won't be interrupted. Sit or lie down in a comfortable position.

2. Close your eyes and take a few deep breaths.

3. Slowly repeat words or phrases in your mind that suggest peace and relaxation. For example, you might say to yourself, "My arms are heavy and warm. My heartbeat is calm and regular."

4. Visualize a peaceful place or experience. Try to involve all your senses.

5. Stay in this relaxed state for a few moments, then slowly bring your awareness back to the present.

Much like the other relaxation techniques, Autogenic Training stimulates the Vagus Nerve, promoting a sense of calm and relaxation. It's a tool for stress relief that you carry with you always, ready to be used whenever you need a moment of calm.

These relaxation techniques, with their focus on body awareness and mindfulness, can effectively stimulate the Vagus Nerve, promoting a sense of calm and well-being. As you explore these techniques, remember to approach them with an attitude of patience and acceptance. It's not about achieving a certain state of relaxation; it's about exploring the landscape of your inner world, appreciating whatever you discover along the way. As you engage with these techniques, you stimulate your Vagus Nerve, inviting calm and relaxation into your life.

6.4 A Personalized Vagus Nerve Exercise Plan

Assessing Your Current Health Status

Before embarking on any new health endeavor, it's vital to pause and take stock of where you currently stand in terms of your health. This can help you understand your unique needs and constraints, inform your goals, and guide your choice of exercises.

Start by reflecting on your current lifestyle. Are you physically active? What does your diet look like? How is your stress level? Also consider any pre-existing health conditions, especially those related to the heart, lungs, or digestive system, as these can significantly impact the function of the Vagus Nerve.

Next, consider your current symptoms. Are you experiencing high levels of anxiety or stress? Do you have issues with your digestion or sleep? Are there any specific health concerns you hope to address by stimulating your Vagus Nerve? By understanding your current state, you can tailor your exercise plan to address these concerns effectively.

Setting Realistic Goals

With a clear understanding of your current health status, you can now move on to setting goals for your Vagus Nerve exercise plan. Remember, the aim here is not perfection, but progress. Your goals should be realistic, achievable, and aligned with your unique needs and capabilities.

Perhaps you aim to reduce your anxiety levels or improve your digestion. Maybe your goal is to enhance your sleep quality or your body's stress response. Whatever your goals may be, ensure they are clear, specific, and measurable. This will not only provide direction for your exercise plan but also offer a tangible way to track your progress.

Choosing Suitable Exercises

Armed with a clear understanding of your health status and goals, you can now select the most suitable exercises for your Vagus Nerve exercise plan. The exercises you choose should align with your goals and be appropriate for your current health status and physical abilities.

Some people might find deep breathing exercises or yoga poses to be most beneficial, while others might prefer relaxation techniques. Also consider the practicality of the exercises. Choose exercises that you can comfortably incorporate into your daily routine and that you enjoy doing.

Remember, the goal is not to do all the exercises, but to find the ones that work best for you. It's about quality, not quantity. By choosing suitable exercises, you not only enhance the effectiveness of your plan but also increase the likelihood of sticking to it.

Tracking Your Progress

Once you've begun your Vagus Nerve exercise plan, it's important to monitor your progress. This can provide valuable feedback, help maintain your motivation, and inform any necessary adjustments to your plan.

Consider keeping a journal to record your exercises, noting any changes in your symptoms, well-being, and overall health. You could also use a heart rate variability monitor to track changes in your Vagus Nerve function.

Remember, progress may be slow, and that's okay. The aim is not to achieve instant results, but to create sustainable changes that enhance your health and well-being over the long term. Celebrate small victories, be patient with setbacks, and most importantly, listen to your body. It's your greatest guide on this path to wellness.

As you implement your personalized Vagus Nerve exercise plan, keep in mind that this is not a one-size-fits-all approach. It's a personalized plan, tailored to your unique needs and goals. It's about fostering a deeper connection with your body, understanding its signals, and responding with care and kindness. With each breath you take, with each pose you hold, with each moment of relaxation, you're not just stimulating your Vagus Nerve; you're embracing a healthier, calmer, and more balanced way of life.

With the knowledge and tools you have gathered, you are well-equipped to navigate the path to Vagus Nerve health. But remember, this is just the beginning. As you continue to explore the vast potential of the Vagus Nerve, you'll discover even more ways to enhance your health and well-being. So, let's keep exploring, keep learning, and most importantly, keep breathing.

CHAPTER 7

Embracing Mindfulness: A Pathway to Vagus Nerve Health

Imagine standing on the shore of a serene lake. You watch as a leaf gently falls onto the surface of the water, creating ripples that spread out in a beautiful pattern. As you observe the leaf, you become aware of the rustling trees, the chirping birds, and the cool breeze on your skin. You're not thinking about the past or worrying about the future; you're simply there, in the moment, fully present and engaged. This, in essence, is the practice of mindfulness.

When we think of improving our health, we often focus on the physical aspects — exercise, diet, sleep. But what if there was another, equally vital aspect we've been overlooking? The mind, much like the body, requires exercise and nurturing. Mindfulness offers a pathway to improve mental fitness, calm the mind, and ultimately, stimulate the Vagus Nerve.

7.1 Introduction to Mindfulness

Definition of Mindfulness

Mindfulness, in its simplest form, is the practice of paying attention in a particular way: on purpose, in the present moment, and nonjudgmentally. It's about observing your thoughts, feelings, sensations, and the world around you without getting caught up in them.

Imagine sitting in a movie theater watching a film. Mindfulness is like stepping back and observing the movie rather than being lost in the plot. You're not trying to change the movie or judge it; you're simply watching it unfold.

Benefits of Mindfulness

The practice of mindfulness, though simple, offers profound benefits for mental, emotional, and physical health.

Mental Health: Mindfulness improves focus and attention, reduces rumination, and enhances cognitive flexibility. It's like decluttering your mind, creating space for clarity, creativity, and problem-solving.

Emotional Health: By observing emotions without judgment, mindfulness helps to regulate emotional responses, reducing reactivity and enhancing resilience. It's akin to being the calm eye in the storm of emotions.

Physical Health: Mindfulness has been found to reduce stress, lower blood pressure, improve sleep, and even alleviate chronic pain. It's like a gentle massage for your nervous system, promoting relaxation and well-being.

Moreover, mindfulness has a direct impact on the Vagus Nerve, stimulating it to promote relaxation, reduce inflammation, and enhance overall health.

Common Misconceptions about Mindfulness

Despite its growing popularity, there are several misconceptions about mindfulness that can create barriers to its practice.

Misconception 1: Mindfulness is about emptying the mind. Many people believe that mindfulness involves clearing the mind of all thoughts. However, mindfulness is not about eliminating thoughts but rather about observing them without judgment. It's about noticing when your mind has wandered and gently bringing it back to the present moment.

Misconception 2: Mindfulness is a time-consuming practice. While regular, dedicated practice can deepen mindfulness, it doesn't need to be time-consuming. Even a few minutes of mindfulness each day can be beneficial. Moreover, mindfulness can be practiced in any moment of the day, whether you're eating, walking, or simply breathing.

Misconception 3: Mindfulness is a religious or spiritual practice. While mindfulness has roots in Buddhist meditation, it's not a religious or spiritual practice. It's a mental training practice that can be beneficial to anyone, regardless of their religious or spiritual beliefs.

Understanding what mindfulness is — and what it's not — can help clear the path to its practice. As we embrace mindfulness, we not only enhance our mental, emotional, and physical health but also stimulate our Vagus Nerve, unlocking the door to enhanced well-being.

7.2 Meditative Practices for Vagus Nerve Stimulation

In the realm of mindfulness, meditation holds a special place. It is like a tranquil oasis, a space where we can pause, breathe, and reconnect with ourselves. But did you know that meditation can also be a powerful tool for stimulating the Vagus Nerve? As we shift our focus inward, we not only enhance our mindfulness but also activate our body's relaxation response, promoting a sense of calm and well-being. Let's explore three meditative practices that can stimulate the Vagus Nerve and enhance our overall health.

Body Scan Meditation

Imagine a gentle wave washing over a sandy beach, touching each grain of sand as it moves. Body Scan Meditation mimics this wave, inviting us to mentally scan our bodies, touching each sensation as we move from head to toe.

To practice Body Scan Meditation:

1. Start by finding a comfortable position, either sitting or lying down. Close your eyes and take a few deep breaths to center yourself.

2. Begin the body scan at the top of your head, bringing your awareness to any sensations you might be feeling.

3. Slowly move your attention down through your body, noticing any feelings of tension, relaxation, warmth, coolness, or anything else that you sense.

4. If you encounter areas of tension, breathe into them, inviting them to relax. However, the goal is not to change or eliminate any sensation but merely to observe it.

5. Continue the scan all the way down to your toes, then spend a few moments experiencing your body as a whole.

This mindful exploration of the body not only enhances our body awareness but also stimulates the Vagus Nerve, promoting a sense of calm and relaxation.

Loving-Kindness Meditation

Picture a pebble dropping into a pond, creating ripples that spread out across the water. Loving-Kindness Meditation creates similar ripples, but the pebble is a silent mantra of well wishes, and the pond is our mind. As we repeat these phrases, we create ripples of positivity, kindness, and compassion.

To practice Loving-Kindness Meditation:

1. Find a comfortable position and close your eyes. Take a few moments to relax your body and quiet your mind.

2. Silently repeat phrases of well wishes for yourself, such as "May I be safe, may I be healthy, may I be happy, may I live with ease." Feel the meaning of these words as you say them.

3. After a few minutes, bring to mind someone you care about. Repeat the phrases of well wishes for this person.

4. Continue this process for other people in your life, including neutral people, difficult people, and finally, all beings everywhere.

Loving-Kindness Meditation not only cultivates positivity and compassion but also stimulates the Vagus Nerve, enhancing our sense of connection and well-being.

Breath Awareness Meditation

Breath, a continuous rhythm of our life, is often taken for granted. Yet, when we tune into this rhythm, we find a powerful tool for mindfulness and relaxation. Breath Awareness Meditation invites us to do just this - to focus our attention on the breath, observing its rhythm, its sensation, its life-giving force.

To practice Breath Awareness Meditation:

1. Choose a comfortable position and close your eyes. Take a moment to settle in.

2. Bring your attention to your breath. Notice the sensation of the breath as it enters and leaves your body.

3. If your mind wanders, gently guide your attention back to your breath, without judgment.

4. Continue for a few minutes, or for as long as it feels comfortable.

Breath Awareness Meditation is a simple yet powerful practice that not only enhances mindfulness but also stimulates the Vagus Nerve. As we tune into our breath, we connect with our body's natural relaxation response, promoting calmness and well-being.

In the garden of mindfulness, meditation blooms like a beautiful flower. Its petals, the practices of body scan, loving-kindness, and breath awareness, offer a path to inner peace and health. As we water this flower with regular practice, we stimulate the Vagus Nerve, inviting its calming influence into our lives. But the growth doesn't stop here. As we continue to nurture this connection, we'll find that the benefits extend beyond the meditation cushion, blooming into all areas of our lives.

7.3 Mindfulness for Stress Management

Mindful Eating

Imagine sitting at your favorite restaurant, a plate of your beloved dish in front of you. You take a bite, the flavors dancing on your tongue, making you close your eyes in delight. You're not just eating; you're experiencing your food, savoring each morsel - this is the essence of mindful eating.

Mindful eating isn't about dieting or depriving yourself. It's about experiencing food more intensely – especially the pleasure of it. You can eat a cheeseburger mindfully, if you wish. You might enjoy it a lot more. Or you might decide, halfway through, that your body has had enough. Or that it really needs some salad.

To practice mindful eating, start by looking at your food. Notice the colors, the shapes, the textures. Now, take a bite. Chew slowly, noticing the flavors, the textures, the temperature. As you swallow, notice the sensation of the food moving down your esophagus and into your stomach. Continue eating this way, bite by bite, fully experiencing your food.

Mindful eating has profound benefits. It can help you enjoy your food more, improve digestion, and even help you recognize your body's hunger and fullness cues. And yes, it can also stimulate the Vagus Nerve, promoting relaxation and improving overall wellness.

Mindful Walking

Picture a path winding through a beautiful forest. As you walk, you feel the crunch of leaves under your feet, the cool breeze on your skin, the sunlight filtering through the trees. You're not just walking; you're connecting with the world around you, step by step - this is mindful walking.

Mindful walking combines the physical act of walking with the mindfulness of the present moment. It's a way to exercise your body and your mind, bringing a sense of peace and relaxation.

To practice mindful walking, start by standing still and becoming aware of your body. Feel the ground under your feet, the air on your skin, the beating of your heart. Now, start to walk. With each step, notice the sensation of movement in your legs, the feeling of your feet touching the ground, the swinging of your arms.

Mindful walking offers a break from the hustle and bustle of daily life. It allows you to enjoy the simple act of walking, to connect with nature, to find peace in the present moment. And yes, it can also stimulate the Vagus Nerve, reducing stress and promoting overall wellness.

Mindful Listening

Imagine sitting in a quiet room, your favorite song playing softly in the background. You close your eyes and let the music wash over you, the melody resonating in your heart, the lyrics touching your soul. You're not just hearing; you're listening, truly listening - this is mindful listening.

Mindful listening involves fully engaging with the sounds around you, whether it's music, the chirping of birds, or the hum of traffic. It's about being fully present with the sound, not thinking about the past or future, not judging or analyzing.

To practice mindful listening, find a quiet place where you can relax. Close your eyes and tune into the sounds around you. It might be the ticking of a clock, the rustling of leaves, the distant sound of traffic. Whatever it is, just listen, fully and completely.

Mindful listening can open up a whole new world of sounds that you may not have noticed before. It can help you stay in the present moment, reduce stress, and enhance your connection with the world around you. And yes, it can also stimulate the Vagus Nerve, promoting a sense of calm and reducing anxiety.

In the symphony of life, mindfulness strikes a harmonious chord, creating a melody of peace and relaxation. With practices like mindful eating, walking, and listening, you can tune into this melody, engaging your mind, your body, and your Vagus Nerve. As you continue to practice mindfulness, you'll discover a new way of living, a way that embraces the present, reduces stress, and promotes overall wellness.

So, take a deep breath, tune into your senses, and step into the world of mindfulness. A world of peace, balance, and well-being awaits you.

7.4 The Role of Mindfulness in Holistic Health

Life, at times, can feel like a whirlwind of tasks, responsibilities, and experiences. Amidst the hustle and bustle, the mind can become noisy, cluttered with thoughts, worries, and stresses. Here's where mindfulness can serve as an anchor, grounding us back into the present moment and bringing a sense of balance and tranquility.

Mindfulness and Mental Health

Picture a busy street in the heart of a bustling city. Cars honking, people rushing, neon signs flashing - a constant stream of noise and activity. Now, imagine being able to find a quiet spot amidst the chaos, a space where you can breathe, observe, and just be. This is what mindfulness can bring to our mental landscape.

Mindfulness is like a mental workout that strengthens our ability to focus, manage our thoughts, and maintain mental clarity. It encourages us to observe our thoughts without judgment, thereby reducing the power they have over our mental state. This can be particularly beneficial when dealing with negative or anxious thoughts. Instead of getting entangled in them, we learn to see them as passing events, reducing their impact on our mental well-being.

Moreover, mindfulness fosters a greater sense of self-awareness and understanding. By tuning into our inner thoughts, feelings, and patterns, we can gain valuable insights into ourselves, enhancing our self-understanding and personal growth.

Mindfulness and Physical Health

Consider a tree standing tall and firm. It's not rigid or unyielding; instead, it sways flexibly with the wind, its roots firmly grounded. This is the state of balance and resilience that mindfulness can help cultivate in our physical health.

Research has shown that mindfulness can have tangible benefits on various aspects of physical health. It can lower blood pressure, reduce chronic pain, improve sleep, and even alleviate gastrointestinal difficulties. These benefits are likely due to the stress-reducing effects of mindfulness. By helping to calm the mind, mindfulness can promote relaxation in the body, positively impacting various physical functions.

Mindfulness also encourages a healthier relationship with our bodies. It cultivates body awareness, helping us tune into our body's signals for hunger, fullness, tiredness, or discomfort. This can lead to healthier lifestyle choices, such as better dietary habits, regular physical activity, and adequate rest.

Mindfulness and Emotional Health

Imagine a sky filled with clouds. Some clouds are fluffy and light, others heavy and dark. But regardless of their shape or size, they all pass across the sky, constantly changing and shifting. Our emotions are like these clouds. They come and go, each one a temporary visitor in the vast sky of our inner world.

Mindfulness invites us to observe our emotional clouds without getting lost in them. It encourages us to feel our emotions fully, whether pleasant or unpleasant, without clinging to them or pushing them away. This can lead to better emotional regulation and greater emotional resilience.

Moreover, mindfulness can enhance our capacity for compassion and empathy, both towards ourselves and others. By being present with our own emotions, we learn to approach them with kindness and understanding. This can then extend to our interactions with others, fostering healthier relationships and greater emotional well-being.

Holistic health, like a beautifully woven tapestry, is made up of multiple threads - mental, physical, and emotional health. Mindfulness acts as a golden thread, running through and connecting all aspects of our health. By weaving mindfulness into our lives, we not only enhance our mental, physical, and emotional well-being but also stimulate the Vagus Nerve, promoting a sense of calm, balance, and overall wellness.

As we conclude this exploration of mindfulness, let's remember that mindfulness is not a destination but a way of journeying through life. It's a practice of returning, again and again, to the present moment, to the here and now. And in this present moment, we can find a sense of peace, balance, and connection - with ourselves, with others, and with the world around us. So, let's step into the now, breathe deeply, and embrace the power of mindfulness. A journey of health, well-being, and discovery awaits us.

CHAPTER 8

Biohacking the Vagus Nerve: Your Blueprint for Optimal Health

Imagine being an architect, designing the blueprint of an innovative building. You meticulously plan each aspect - the foundation, the structure, the materials - ensuring that the building stands tall and strong. Now consider your health as this building; biohacking is the skill that allows you to be your own architect, to design and optimize your health blueprint. In this chapter, we delve into the fascinating world of biohacking - what it is, its benefits, and its implications for the Vagus Nerve.

8.1 Introduction to Biohacking

Definition of Biohacking

Biohacking, in essence, is the practice of changing our chemistry and our physiology through science and self-experimentation to energize and enhance our bodies. It's about making your body function better by applying the principles of biology (hence the term 'bio'), coupled with hacking, a term used in the tech world to refer to finding innovative and efficient ways to perform tasks.

From changing your diet to manipulating your sleep patterns, to incorporating specific exercises into your routine, biohacking encompasses a wide range of activities. But at its core, it's about understanding and applying the science behind how our bodies function to improve our physical, mental, and emotional health.

Benefits of Biohacking

Biohacking can yield a multitude of benefits, depending largely upon the strategies and techniques you choose to employ. Here are a few potential outcomes:

- Enhanced Physical Health: Through diet modifications, high-intensity interval training (HIIT), and other physical health hacks, biohackers can improve their strength, endurance, and overall fitness.

- Improved Cognitive Performance: Certain biohacks aim to boost mental clarity, focus, and memory. This can be achieved through various means, such as brain-training exercises, nootropics (substances that may improve cognitive function), and mindfulness practices.

- Optimized Emotional Well-being: By employing techniques such as deep breathing exercises, yoga, and other stress-reducing activities, biohackers can enhance their emotional health, leading to better stress management and improved emotional balance.

- Augmented Sleep Quality: Biohacking techniques such as sleep tracking, sleep hygiene practices, and circadian rhythm alignment can lead to deeper, more restful sleep, which is crucial for overall health and well-being.

- Personal Empowerment: Perhaps one of the most impactful benefits of biohacking is the sense of empowerment it brings. Biohacking puts you in the driver's seat of your own health, empowering you to make informed decisions that directly impact your health and wellness.

Risks and Ethical Considerations in Biohacking

While biohacking holds promise for improved health and wellness, it's not without its risks and ethical considerations. Here are a few points to ponder:

- Lack of Regulation: Many biohacking tools and supplements are not regulated by health authorities like the FDA, which means their safety and efficacy may not be guaranteed.

- Potential Health Risks: Some biohacking techniques may carry health risks, especially if carried out without proper knowledge or supervision. For instance, extreme dietary changes can lead to nutrient deficiencies or other health problems.

- Privacy Concerns: Certain biohacking techniques involve tracking and sharing health data, which could potentially be exploited if not properly protected.

- Ethical Considerations: Biohacking also raises ethical questions. For instance, if certain biohacks can enhance cognitive or physical abilities beyond what's considered 'normal,' who gets access to these enhancements? And could this lead to unfair advantages or disparities?

In the realm of biohacking, the Vagus Nerve presents itself as a key player. By understanding and manipulating its functions, we can 'hack' our way to improved health and wellness. As we continue to explore this innovative field, we'll uncover how biohacking and the Vagus Nerve intersect, and how this intersection can lead us to the path of optimal health. But for now, let's dive a little deeper into the world of biohacking - a world where science, self-experimentation, and health converge into a blueprint for optimal living.

8.2 Biohacking Techniques for Vagus Nerve Health

Cold Exposure

Have you ever stepped outside on a frosty morning and felt your body instinctively react to the cold? This automatic response is a part of your body's intricate survival mechanisms. One key player in these reactions is the Vagus Nerve, which is stimulated during cold exposure.

When you expose your body to cold, the Vagus Nerve springs into action, initiating various responses such as constriction of blood vessels in your skin and extremities, and an increase in your heart rate. This is your body's way of preserving core body temperature. As a bonus, this stimulation of the Vagus Nerve can also help to reduce inflammation, enhance mood, and boost overall resilience.

Practically, you can incorporate cold exposure into your routine by taking cold showers, immersing your face in cold water, or spending time in cold environments. Always remember to listen to your body and not push beyond your comfort levels.

Intermittent Fasting

Think about how you feel after a large meal. Often, there's a sense of heaviness and sluggishness, as your body diverts energy towards digestion. Now, imagine the opposite situation - the state of fasting. This is a state of lightness and heightened alertness, where the body switches from digestion to other processes such as repair and rejuvenation.

Intermittent fasting, which involves cycling between periods of eating and fasting, taps into this state.

When you fast, your body shifts into a 'rest and repair' mode, which involves a cascade of processes that are mediated by the Vagus Nerve. These include enhancing the body's stress resilience, promoting cellular repair processes, and improving insulin sensitivity.

You can practice intermittent fasting in various ways, such as the 16/8 method (fasting for 16 hours and eating only during an 8-hour window), or the 5:2 method (eating normally for five days of the week and restricting calories for two days). It's essential to choose a method that suits your lifestyle and health needs, and as always, consult with a healthcare professional if needed.

High-Intensity Interval Training (HIIT)

Picturing a roller coaster ride, with its thrilling highs and lows, gives you a sense of what High-Intensity Interval Training (HIIT) involves. It's a form of exercise that alternates between intense bursts of activity and fixed periods of less-intense activity or even complete rest.

This variation in intensity not only makes the workout challenging and exciting but also holds several benefits for your health, including improved cardiovascular fitness, enhanced fat burning, and better blood sugar regulation. Furthermore, the intense effort followed by rest stimulates the Vagus Nerve, enhancing its tone and function.

A HIIT workout may include a variety of exercises, such as sprinting, cycling, jump roping, or bodyweight exercises, and can be easily adapted to suit your fitness level and preferences. Remember, the key to HIIT is the alternation between high and low intensity, pushing your limits but also allowing your body to recover.

The realm of biohacking presents a myriad of techniques to optimize health and well-being. By exploring and incorporating methods such as cold exposure, intermittent fasting, and high-intensity interval training, you're not only enhancing your physical performance but also stimulating your Vagus Nerve. This stimulation holds the key to unlocking numerous health benefits, from reduced inflammation to improved mood to enhanced resilience. As you experiment with these techniques, remember to respect your body's signals and embrace the process of self-discovery and optimization.

8.3 Measuring the Effectiveness of Your Biohacking Efforts

Without a yardstick to measure progress, any journey can feel like wandering in the dark. In the realm of biohacking, this yardstick takes the form of specific markers and metrics that provide tangible evidence of progress and effectiveness. By tracking these markers, you can make informed decisions, fine-tune your strategies, and visualize your path towards optimal health. Let's explore three key metrics that can help measure the effectiveness of your biohacking efforts.

Tracking Your Heart Rate Variability (HRV)

Imagine the rhythm of your heart as a beautiful piece of music. In this symphony of life, the tempo is not constant; there's a slight variation in the time interval between beats. This variation, known as Heart Rate Variability (HRV), serves as a window into your body's state of balance, stress resilience, and overall health.

HRV is predominantly regulated by the Vagus Nerve, which, when stimulated, can increase HRV, indicating a healthier and more resilient body. By tracking your HRV, you can gain insights into the effectiveness of your biohacking efforts. A rise in HRV over time could indicate that your Vagus Nerve is being effectively stimulated, and your body is adapting positively to your biohacking interventions.

Several devices and apps, such as heart rate monitors and fitness trackers, can help you track your HRV. Regular tracking can provide valuable data, guiding your biohacking journey and providing motivation to stay on the course.

Monitoring Your Sleep Quality

Sleep, the sweet balm that soothes and restores our bodies, is a cornerstone of good health. The quality of your sleep can speak volumes about the state of your health and the effectiveness of your biohacking efforts.

Quality sleep involves cycling through various stages, each with its unique restorative functions. Any disruptions to this cycle, such as trouble falling asleep, frequent awakenings, or lack of deep sleep, can affect your health and well-being.

Many biohacking techniques aim to improve sleep quality, as better sleep often translates to improved health. Monitoring your sleep, therefore, can provide insights into the effectiveness of these techniques. Are you falling asleep faster? Are you waking up less during the night? Are you feeling refreshed upon waking? The answers to these questions can help gauge the success of your biohacking strategies.

Various tools can assist in tracking sleep quality, from wearable devices to smartphone apps that monitor your movements and sounds during the night. Regular monitoring can provide a wealth of information, helping you understand your sleep patterns and make necessary adjustments to your biohacking plan.

Assessing Your Mental Clarity and Focus

Just as a foggy morning obscures the beauty of a sunrise, lack of mental clarity can cloud our lives, making it difficult to focus, make decisions, or think creatively. Mental clarity and focus, therefore, serve as crucial indicators of brain health and overall well-being.

Many biohacking techniques focus on enhancing cognitive functions, such as mental clarity, memory, and focus. By assessing these functions, you can gauge the effectiveness of these techniques. Are you finding it easier to concentrate? Are you feeling more mentally alert? Are you experiencing less brain fog? The answers to these questions can indicate whether your biohacking efforts are paying off.

Various cognitive tests and self-assessment tools can help you measure your mental clarity and focus. Regular assessment can provide a clear picture of your cognitive health, helping you fine-tune your biohacking strategies for optimal results.

In the quest for optimal health, these metrics serve as guiding stars, illuminating the path and providing feedback on our progress. By tracking your Heart Rate Variability, monitoring your sleep quality, and assessing your mental clarity and focus, you can measure the effectiveness of your biohacking efforts. This not only ensures that you're moving in the right direction but also empowers you to take charge of your health journey. And as you continue this journey, remember, every step you take brings you closer to your goal of optimal health. So, keep tracking, keep adjusting, and most importantly, keep going.

8.4 Biohacking Success Stories

Case Study: Overcoming Anxiety with Biohacking

Consider the story of Lisa, a 35-year-old software engineer who had been grappling with anxiety for several years. Her demanding job and high-pressure environment kept her on a constant adrenaline rush. She often experienced heart palpitations, sleepless nights, and overwhelming feelings of worry.

Determined to regain control over her life, Lisa turned to biohacking. She started with small, manageable changes to her lifestyle. She incorporated a daily meditation practice, focusing on her breath to calm her racing thoughts. She also adjusted her diet, adding more omega-3 fatty acids and probiotics to nourish her gut, an essential aspect of mental health.

But the most significant change came when she began using cold exposure therapy. Every morning, Lisa would end her shower with a minute of cold water. Though challenging at first, she soon noticed a marked decrease in her anxiety levels. The cold showers, acting as a form of stress, trained her body to better handle her day-to-day anxiety.

Over time, these biohacking techniques helped Lisa manage her anxiety effectively. She reported feeling more relaxed, her sleep improved, and her heart palpitations decreased significantly. Lisa's story is a testament to the transformative power of biohacking in managing anxiety.

Case Study: Enhancing Physical Performance through Biohacking

Now, let's look at the case of Tom, a passionate amateur cyclist. Tom loved the thrill of competition but often found himself struggling to keep up with his teammates. He suffered from frequent muscle cramps, fatigue, and slow recovery times.

Intrigued by the concept of biohacking, Tom decided to give it a shot. He started with high-intensity interval training (HIIT), pushing his body to its limits in short bursts of intense exercise, followed by periods of rest.

Tom also experimented with intermittent fasting, restricting his eating window to eight hours each day. This eating pattern, he found, helped maintain his energy levels and aided in faster recovery post-workout.

But the most impactful biohack for Tom was tracking his heart rate variability (HRV). By monitoring this metric, he could tailor his training schedule based on his body's readiness, preventing overtraining and enhancing performance.

Over several months, Tom noticed dramatic improvements in his cycling performance. He had more energy, his muscle cramps reduced, and his recovery time quickened. Tom's experience illustrates the potential of biohacking techniques in enhancing physical performance and endurance.

Case Study: Achieving Optimal Health with Biohacking

Finally, let's explore the story of Maria, a 45-year-old teacher. Though not suffering from any particular health issue, Maria often felt tired and lacked energy. She wanted to improve her overall health and vitality.

Maria embarked on her biohacking adventure by making changes to her diet. She prioritized whole, nutrient-dense foods and eliminated processed, sugary foods. She also started practicing yoga, focusing on poses that stimulate the Vagus Nerve.

Additionally, Maria incorporated a mindfulness practice into her daily routine, spending a few minutes each day in quiet contemplation. She also ensured she was getting quality sleep every night, understanding its critical role in overall health.

These biohacks transformed Maria's health. She reported having more energy throughout the day, her sleep improved, and she felt more calm and focused. Maria's journey illustrates how biohacking can lead to improved overall health and well-being.

The stories of Lisa, Tom, and Maria highlight the potential of biohacking in addressing various health concerns - from anxiety to physical performance to overall health. These are not just stories of health transformation, but also of empowerment. Through biohacking, these individuals took control of their own health, experimenting, learning, and discovering what works best for them.

As we turn the page to the next chapter, we'll continue to explore the vast potential of the Vagus Nerve, learning more about how to nurture this essential nerve for optimal health and well-being. The journey to better health is a marathon, not a sprint. But with tools like biohacking, we can make the journey more efficient, effective, and rewarding.

CHAPTER 9

Cultivating a Vagus Nerve-Friendly Lifestyle: Your Path to Wellness

---

Welcome to the pivotal chapter of our journey—where theory transforms into action, and understanding becomes a lifestyle. Cultivating a Vagus nerve-friendly lifestyle is your key to unlocking enduring wellness and embracing life with tranquility. Let's dive into practical ways to nurture your Vagus nerve and foster a profound sense of well-being.

Mindful Moments: Embrace the Present

Begin your day with a few minutes of mindful breathing. Inhale serenity, exhale stress. Engage in activities that captivate your attention—reading, painting, or even savoring a cup of tea. These moments of mindfulness not only relax your mind but also send gentle signals to your Vagus nerve, inviting it to harmonize with your inner calm.

Social Soul-Feeding: Connect Deeply

Nourish your Vagus nerve through meaningful connections. Engage in heartfelt conversations with friends and family. Listen intently, empathize genuinely, and share your thoughts openly. Laughter and shared joy stimulate your Vagus nerve, strengthening your emotional bonds and enhancing your overall resilience.

Feeding Your Body, Feeding Your Nerve: The Vagus Nerve Diet

Craft your meals with your Vagus nerve in mind. Opt for omega-3 rich foods like salmon and walnuts, known to calm inflammation. Embrace the probiotic power of yogurt and kefir, fostering a healthy gut-brain dialogue. Color your plate with vibrant vegetables and fruits, providing essential nutrients for your nerve's vitality.

Restful Nights: Prioritize Sleep

Create a sleep sanctuary. Dim the lights, banish gadgets, and unwind with a calming ritual before bedtime. Adequate sleep not only rejuvenates your body but also fortifies your vagal tone, enabling you to face each day with renewed energy and composure.

Nature's Embrace: Reconnect Outdoors

Take barefoot walks on grass, breathe in the forest air, or simply sit under the sky. Nature's calming influence resonates deeply with your Vagus nerve, grounding you in the present moment and washing away stress.

Gratitude: The Heartfelt Elixir

Practice gratitude daily. Reflect on your blessings, acknowledging even the smallest joys. Gratitude is a profound activator of the Vagus nerve, fostering positive emotions and cultivating resilience.

Loving Kindness: Radiate Compassion

Engage in acts of kindness. Help a neighbor, volunteer, or simply offer a warm smile. Cultivating compassion not only elevates your spirit but also enhances your vagal tone, promoting a sense of interconnectedness and harmony.

As you embrace these practices, remember, it's not about perfection; it's about progress. Each mindful breath, every shared laugh, and every moment of gratitude is a step toward a Vagus nerve-friendly lifestyle. Let these practices become your daily companions, guiding you toward a life infused with balance, resilience, and unshakeable peace. Your journey to wellness starts here, in the choices you make, the connections you foster, and the love you embrace—nurturing not just your Vagus nerve but your entire being.

CHAPTER 10

Overcoming Obstacles on the Path to Vagus Nerve Wellness

Imagine standing at the edge of a vast forest, your eyes tracing the winding path that disappears into the verdant green. You know that this path holds the promise of discovery, adventure, and transformation. Yet, you also know that the journey won't be easy. There will be challenges to face, obstacles to overcome. But with every step, with every challenge you conquer, you grow stronger, more resilient, and closer to your destination.

Such is the journey towards Vagus Nerve health. It's a path of self-discovery, of learning to listen to your body's whispers and respond with care and kindness. It's about understanding the power that lies within your own body - the power to heal, to transform, to thrive. But like any journey, it comes with its own set of challenges. Let's take a closer look at these challenges and explore strategies to overcome them.

10.1 Identifying Challenges in Nurturing the Vagus Nerve

Challenge: Lack of Time

Consider the rush of a typical weekday morning. The alarm clock blares, pulling you out of sleep. There's breakfast to make, emails to check, and a to-do list that seems to stretch on forever. Amidst this rush, finding time for Vagus Nerve exercises can seem like an impossible task.

This lack of time is one of the most common challenges faced by individuals on their path to Vagus Nerve health. In our fast-paced world, where there always seems to be something to do or somewhere to be, carving out time for self-care can often fall by the wayside.

Challenge: Lack of Knowledge

Now, imagine stepping into a vast library, the shelves brimming with books on every conceivable topic. The sheer volume of information can be overwhelming, leaving you unsure of where to start or what to trust.

This is what trying to learn about the Vagus Nerve can feel like for many people.

The Vagus Nerve, with its complex functions and broad influence on health, can be a daunting topic to understand. The lack of accessible and reliable information can lead to confusion, misconceptions, and even fear, posing a significant challenge on the path to Vagus Nerve health.

Challenge: Lack of Motivation

Finally, picture a time when you were excited about starting a new project or habit. The initial enthusiasm was high, and you jumped in with both feet. But as time passed, the excitement waned, and motivation dipped, making it harder and harder to stick to your plan.

Starting a new health regimen, like Vagus Nerve exercises, can trigger a similar pattern. The initial motivation can be high, but maintaining this motivation over time can be challenging. This lack of sustained motivation is a common obstacle to maintaining the consistent practice needed for Vagus Nerve health.

The challenges of lack of time, lack of knowledge, and lack of motivation may seem formidable. But remember, every challenge presents an opportunity for growth and transformation. By understanding these challenges and equipping ourselves with effective strategies to overcome them, we can navigate the path towards Vagus Nerve health with confidence and resilience. So, let's lace up our boots, step onto the path, and start this exciting journey towards greater health and well-being.

10.2 Strategies to Overcome these Challenges

Strategy for Overcoming Lack of Time

Think about your day as a canvas, each hour a stroke of paint adding depth and texture to your masterpiece. Each stroke is vital, shaping the final piece. Time, indeed, is one of our most valuable and finite resources. When the challenge of time scarcity presents itself, consider the following strategies.

Prioritize and Plan

Start by identifying your priorities. What are the non-negotiable aspects of your day? Where can you create pockets of time for your Vagus nerve exercises? Spend a few minutes at the start of your day or week to plan. A little planning can go a long way in helping you manage your time more effectively and ensure that your wellness practices are not compromised.

Integrate Exercises into Your Daily Routine

Vagus nerve exercises don't necessarily require a dedicated slot in your schedule. Many of these exercises, such as deep breathing or mindfulness, can be integrated into your existing routine. For example, try performing deep breathing exercises while commuting or practice mindfulness while doing household chores.

Start Small

Remember, it's not about the length of time you dedicate but the consistency of your practice. Start with small, manageable chunks of time - even a few minutes a day can make a difference. As you cultivate the habit, you can gradually increase the duration of your practice.

Strategy for Overcoming Lack of Knowledge

In the vast ocean of information, it's easy to feel adrift, unsure of where to sail. If lack of knowledge is your challenge, consider these strategies.

Educate Yourself

Start by gaining a basic understanding of the Vagus nerve - its functions, its role in health, and ways to enhance its function. There are numerous resources available, from books to online courses to informative websites, that can offer valuable insights.

Consult Professionals

Health professionals, such as doctors, therapists, or wellness coaches, can provide reliable and personalized advice. Don't hesitate to reach out and ask questions. After all, every question you ask is a step towards greater knowledge and understanding.

Join Communities

There are numerous online and offline communities where you can connect with others on a similar journey. These communities can offer support, share resources, and provide a space for you to learn and grow.

Strategy for Overcoming Lack of Motivation

Motivation, like a garden, requires regular nurturing. If you find your motivation waning, these strategies might help.

Set Realistic Goals

Having clear, achievable goals can fuel your motivation. Whether it's improving digestion, reducing anxiety, or enhancing sleep quality, having a specific goal gives you a direction and a purpose.

Celebrate Progress

Every step you take towards your goal, no matter how small, is worth celebrating. Acknowledge your progress, reward yourself for your efforts, and use your success to fuel further motivation.

Stay Flexible

Your path to Vagus nerve health doesn't have to be rigid. It's okay to experiment, to try new exercises, to adjust your goals. Remaining flexible can keep the journey interesting and help sustain your motivation.

In the face of challenges, remember, you are a warrior, equipped with the shield of knowledge, the sword of strategies, and the armor of resilience. With these tools, you can navigate the path towards Vagus nerve health, overcoming obstacles, and moving closer to your goal with each step. So, take a deep breath, tighten your grip, and step forward. The path awaits, and so does the promise of health and wellness.

10.3 Maintaining Motivation in Your Vagus Nerve Health Journey

Celebrating Small Wins

Imagine standing at the base of a towering mountain, the peak lost in the clouds. The climb seems daunting, perhaps even impossible. But then, you shift your gaze to the path before you, to the small stones and pebbles lining the way. You pick up a pebble, admire its unique shape and texture, and take your first step. That's the essence of celebrating small wins on your path to Vagus Nerve health.

Each small win - be it waking up feeling rested, noticing a drop in your anxiety levels, or simply remembering to breathe deeply during a stressful moment - is a pebble on your path. It's a sign that you're moving forward, that you're making progress.

So, don't wait until you've reached the peak to celebrate. Revel in the joy of each pebble picked, each step taken. This not only enhances your motivation but also makes the journey more enjoyable.

Finding a Support Group

Now, picture yourself on the mountain trail again. This time, you're not alone. You are part of a group, each member cheering the others on, sharing stories, offering a helping hand when the path gets steep. This is the power of finding a support group on your Vagus Nerve health journey.

A support group can be a safe space to share your experiences, challenges, and victories. It can provide encouragement, advice, and most importantly, the reassurance that you're not alone. You are part of a community, a team working towards a common goal.

Whether it's an online forum, a local wellness group, or even a group of friends or family members, finding your tribe can be a powerful motivator. It reminds you that you are part of something bigger, that your journey matters not just to you, but also to others.

Finally, imagine reaching a resting point on your mountain climb. You sit down, pull out a journal, and start jotting down the day's experiences - the distance covered, the challenges faced, the beautiful sights witnessed. This is akin to keeping a progress journal on your Vagus Nerve health journey.

A progress journal is a tangible record of your journey. It's a place to note down your exercises, record your feelings, track your progress. It allows you to see how far you've come, to notice patterns, to acknowledge your efforts.

As you fill the pages of your journal, you're not just recording your journey; you're also reinforcing your motivation. You're reminding yourself of your commitment, your resilience, your progress. You're telling the story of your journey towards Vagus Nerve health, one entry at a time.

The path to Vagus Nerve health, like any worthwhile pursuit, requires motivation. It requires the ability to celebrate small wins, to find support in a community, to record your progress. It's about finding joy in each step, appreciating the companionship on the path, cherishing the story that unfolds with each journal entry. So, hold on to these tools of motivation as you continue your climb towards the peak of Vagus Nerve health. The view from the top will be worth every step.

10.4 The Impact of Aging on the Vagus Nerve

Imagine a tree, standing tall and majestic in the heart of a forest. As the years pass, the tree grows older. Its bark becomes rougher, its leaves change colors, and some branches may even lose their strength. But no matter the changes, the tree continues to stand, resilient and enduring. Aging, a natural process, brings about similar changes in our bodies, including the Vagus Nerve.

As we age, our bodies undergo various physiological changes. These changes, influenced by factors like genetics, lifestyle, and environment, also affect the function of our nervous system, including the Vagus Nerve. Research suggests that the efficiency of the Vagus Nerve may decline with age, potentially leading to decreased heart rate variability, increased inflammatory response, and a higher risk of various health disorders.

This does not mean that aging is a downward spiral. It merely signifies that as we add more candles to our birthday cake, our approach to nurturing the Vagus Nerve may need some adjustments.

Strategies for Maintaining Vagus Nerve Health as You Age

The key to aging gracefully lies in adaptation. It's about understanding the changes that come with age and adjusting our lifestyle to accommodate these changes. Here are some strategies that can help maintain Vagus Nerve health as you age.

Regular Physical Activity

Engaging in regular physical activity is crucial at any age, and it's especially beneficial as we grow older. Exercise helps maintain cardiovascular health, supports cognitive function, and boosts mood - all of which are linked to Vagus Nerve function. Choose activities that you enjoy and that suit your fitness level. It could be a daily walk in the park, a yoga class, or even dancing.

Balanced Nutrition

As we age, our nutritional needs change. It's important to fuel our bodies with a balanced diet rich in fruits, vegetables, lean proteins, and whole grains. These nutrient-rich foods support overall health and Vagus Nerve function. Also, consider including fermented foods in your diet to support gut health, which is closely tied to the Vagus Nerve.

Adequate Rest and Relaxation

Rest and relaxation are vital for health at any age. As we get older, ensuring we get quality sleep and regular relaxation becomes even more important. Establish a regular sleep schedule, create a relaxing bedtime routine, and engage in relaxation techniques like deep breathing or meditation to stimulate the Vagus Nerve.

Case Study: Enhancing Vagus Nerve Health in Older Adults

Let's consider the example of John, a 70-year-old retired banker. Even though he was in good health, he often felt tired and experienced occasional digestive issues. Upon learning about the Vagus Nerve and its impact on health, John decided to try some exercises to stimulate it.

John started with deep breathing exercises. Every morning, after his daily walk, he would sit quietly and practice deep, rhythmic breathing for a few minutes. He also incorporated mindfulness into his routine, taking moments throughout the day to focus on his breath and surroundings.

To address his digestive issues, John made some changes to his diet. He started eating more fiber-rich foods, reduced his intake of processed foods, and added a serving of yogurt to his daily meals to support his gut health.

Over time, John noticed a significant improvement in his energy levels and digestion. He also reported feeling calmer and more focused. This case study illustrates that age is not a barrier to enhancing Vagus Nerve health. With consistent practice and lifestyle adjustments, you can maintain and even improve Vagus Nerve function in your golden years.As the sun sets on this chapter, let's remember that aging, like the setting sun, is a natural part of life. It brings changes, yes, but also the beauty of wisdom, experience, and maturity. By understanding these changes and adapting our lifestyle, we can continue to nurture our Vagus Nerve and support our overall health. So, as we step into the golden years of our life, let's do so with grace, wisdom, and an unwavering commitment to our well-being. The journey continues, and so does our exploration of the Vagus Nerve and its incredible potential.

Conclusion

As we reach the end of this profound exploration into the world of the Vagus Nerve, it feels like we've been on a remarkable journey together. We've traversed through the intricate pathways of our nervous system, uncovering the significant role of the Vagus Nerve in our overall health and well-being.

This longest cranial nerve, as we've discovered, holds immense power in its subtle, rhythmic actions. It's the calm conductor orchestrating our "rest and digest" functions, the gentle regulator of our heartbeats, and the critical link in the mind-body connection. The importance of the Vagus Nerve, as we've learned, cannot be overstated.

Along the way, we have gleaned key strategies to nurture and stimulate this vital nerve. From deep breathing exercises and yoga poses to a balanced diet and quality sleep, each strategy is a piece of the puzzle, contributing to the picture of optimal Vagus Nerve health. And let's not forget the role of our environment and lifestyle in supporting the health of this magnificent nerve.

At this point, I want to pause and acknowledge you for the time and dedication you've put into understanding this complex topic. Your curiosity and commitment are testaments to your resilience and dedication to enhancing your health. But remember, this book is just the beginning. The world of the Vagus Nerve is vast and continually evolving, and I encourage you to continue learning, exploring, and practicing.

As we wrap up, I want to leave you with a final thought. The journey to Vagus Nerve health is not a sprint; it's a marathon. It's a path that requires patience, consistency, and above all, kindness towards oneself. There will be days when the progress seems slow, when old habits creep in, or when motivation wanes. But on those days, take a deep breath, remind yourself of why you started, and remember - every small step counts.

As you continue on this journey, know that you are not alone. I am with you, cheering you on, sharing in your victories, and learning from your experiences. Together, let's continue to explore, to grow, and to journey towards optimal health and well-being. Because at the end of the day, it's not just about the destination; it's about the journey, the learning, the growth, and the transformation. It's about becoming the best version of ourselves, one deep breath at a time.

Here's to our health, to the incredible Vagus Nerve, and to the amazing journey ahead.

References

- *Neuroanatomy, Cranial Nerve 10 (Vagus Nerve) - StatPearls* https://www.ncbi.nlm.nih.gov/books/NBK537171/

- *Vagus Nerve as Modulator of the Brain–Gut Axis in ...* https://www.ncbi.nlm.nih.gov/pmc/articles/PMC5859128/

- *Vagus Nerve as Modulator of the Brain–Gut Axis in Psychiatric ...* https://www.ncbi.nlm.nih.gov/pmc/articles/PMC5859128/#:~:text=The%20vagus%20nerve%20represents%20the,%2C%20digestion%2C%20and%20heart%20rate.

- *The Vagus Nerve in the Neuro-Immune Axis* https://www.ncbi.nlm.nih.gov/pmc/articles/PMC5673632/

- *Vagus Nerve as Modulator of the Brain–Gut Axis in ...* https://www.frontiersin.org/articles/10.3389/fpsyt.2018.00044

- *How to Stimulate Your Vagus Nerve for Better Mental
  Health* https://sass.uottawa.ca/sites/sass.uottawa.
  ca/files/how_to_stimulate_your_vagus_nerve_fo
  r_better_mental_health_1.pdf

- *Vagus Nerve Stimulation Modulates Complexity of
  Heart*
  ... https://www.ncbi.nlm.nih.gov/pmc/articles/P
  MC5682746/

- *Fear and anxiety take a double hit from vagal nerve*
  ... https://www.ncbi.nlm.nih.gov/pmc/articles/P
  MC4176918/

- *Vagus Nerve as Modulator of the Brain–Gut Axis in*
  ... https://www.frontiersin.org/articles/10.3389/fp
  syt.2018.00044

- *Role of the Vagus nerve in the development and
  treatment*
  ... https://www.ncbi.nlm.nih.gov/pmc/articles/P
  MC5063945/

- *Effect of Probiotics on Central Nervous System
  Functions in*
  ... https://www.ncbi.nlm.nih.gov/pmc/articles/P
  MC5056568/

- *Vagus Nerve and Underlying Impact on the Gut Microbiota*
... https://www.ncbi.nlm.nih.gov/pmc/articles/PMC9656367/

- *Autonomic Dysfunction in Sleep Disorders* https://www.ncbi.nlm.nih.gov/pmc/articles/PMC8926769/

- *Autonomic Dysfunction in Sleep Disorders* https://www.ncbi.nlm.nih.gov/pmc/articles/PMC8926769/

- *Transcutaneous Vagus Nerve Stimulation Could Improve*
... https://www.ncbi.nlm.nih.gov/pmc/articles/PMC9599790/

- *Effects of Vagus Nerve Stimulation on Sleep-Disordered*
... https://www.ncbi.nlm.nih.gov/pmc/articles/PMC9163944/

- *The Vagus nerve and the inflammatory reflex — linking*
... https://www.ncbi.nlm.nih.gov/pmc/articles/PMC4082307/

- *Vagus Nerve Stimulation and the Cardiovascular System* https://pubmed.ncbi.nlm.nih.gov/31109966/

- *Role of vagus nerve stimulation in the treatment of chronic*
  ... https://pubmed.ncbi.nlm.nih.gov/37369181/

- *The Vagus Nerve in Lung Disease - Jerry Yu* https://grantome.com/grant/NIH/I01-BX003274-02

- *Breath of Life: The Respiratory Vagal Stimulation Model*
  ... https://www.ncbi.nlm.nih.gov/pmc/articles/PMC6189422/

- *6 Vagus Nerve Exercises to Boost Your Well-being* https://yogauonline.com/yoga-practice-teaching-tips/yoga-practice-tips/6-ways-to-stimulate-your-vagus-nerve-with-yoga-and-breathing/

- *How to Stimulate Your Vagus Nerve for Better Mental Health* https://sass.uottawa.ca/sites/sass.uottawa.ca/files/how_to_stimulate_your_vagus_nerve_for_better_mental_health_1.pdf

- *Vagus Nerve Stimulation How-To (And 8 Exercises to*
  Try) https://www.parsleyhealth.com/blog/how-to-stimulate-vagus-nerve-exercises/

- *Breath of Life: The Respiratory Vagal Stimulation Model*
  ... https://www.ncbi.nlm.nih.gov/pmc/articles/PMC6189422/

- *Mindfulness Meditation and the Vagus Nerve Share Many*
  ... https://www.psychologytoday.com/us/blog/the-athletes-way/201602/mindfulness-meditation-and-the-vagus-nerve-share-many-powers

- *Mindfulness meditation: A research-proven way to reduce*
  stress https://www.apa.org/topics/mindfulness/meditation#:~:text=Researchers%20believe%20the%20benefits%20of,downstream%20effects%20throughout%20the%20body.

- *Meditation and Mindfulness: What You Need To Know |*
  NCCIH https://www.nccih.nih.gov/health/meditation-and-mindfulness-what-you-need-to-know

- *Biohacking: What is it, types and hacks to try for beginners* https://www.medicalnewstoday.com/articles/biohacking

- *Biohacking 101: Hack Your Nervous System* https://neuvanalife.com/blogs/blog/biohacking-101-hack-your-nervous-system

- *Methods of assessing vagus nerve activity and reflexes* https://www.ncbi.nlm.nih.gov/pmc/articles/PMC4322860/

- *I'm 32 and spent $200k on biohacking. Became calmer ...* https://hackernoon.com/im-32-and-spent-200k-on-biohacking-became-calmer-thinner-extroverted-healthier-happier-2a2e846ae113

- *Sleep deprivation reduces vagal tone during an inspiratory* ... https://pubmed.ncbi.nlm.nih.gov/33895822/

- *Both high fat and high carbohydrate diets impair vagus* ... https://www.ncbi.nlm.nih.gov/pmc/articles/PMC8128917/

- *Exercise activates vagal induction of dopamine and* ... https://www.ncbi.nlm.nih.gov/pmc/articles/PMC6334665/

- *Vagus Nerve as Modulator of the Brain–Gut Axis in* ... https://www.ncbi.nlm.nih.gov/pmc/articles/PMC5859128/

- *Effects of Aging on the Responsiveness of the Human* ... https://www.ahajournals.org/doi/full/10.1161/01.cir.91.2.351

- *19 Factors That May Stimulate Your Vagus Nerve Naturally* https://health.selfdecode.com/blog/32-ways-to-stimulate-your-vagus-nerve-and-all-you-need-to-know-about-it/

- *The vagus nerve and the inflammatory reflex — linking* ... https://www.ncbi.nlm.nih.gov/pmc/articles/PMC4082307/

- *Vagus Nerve as Modulator of the Brain–Gut Axis in* ... https://www.frontiersin.org/articles/10.3389/fpsyt.2018.00044